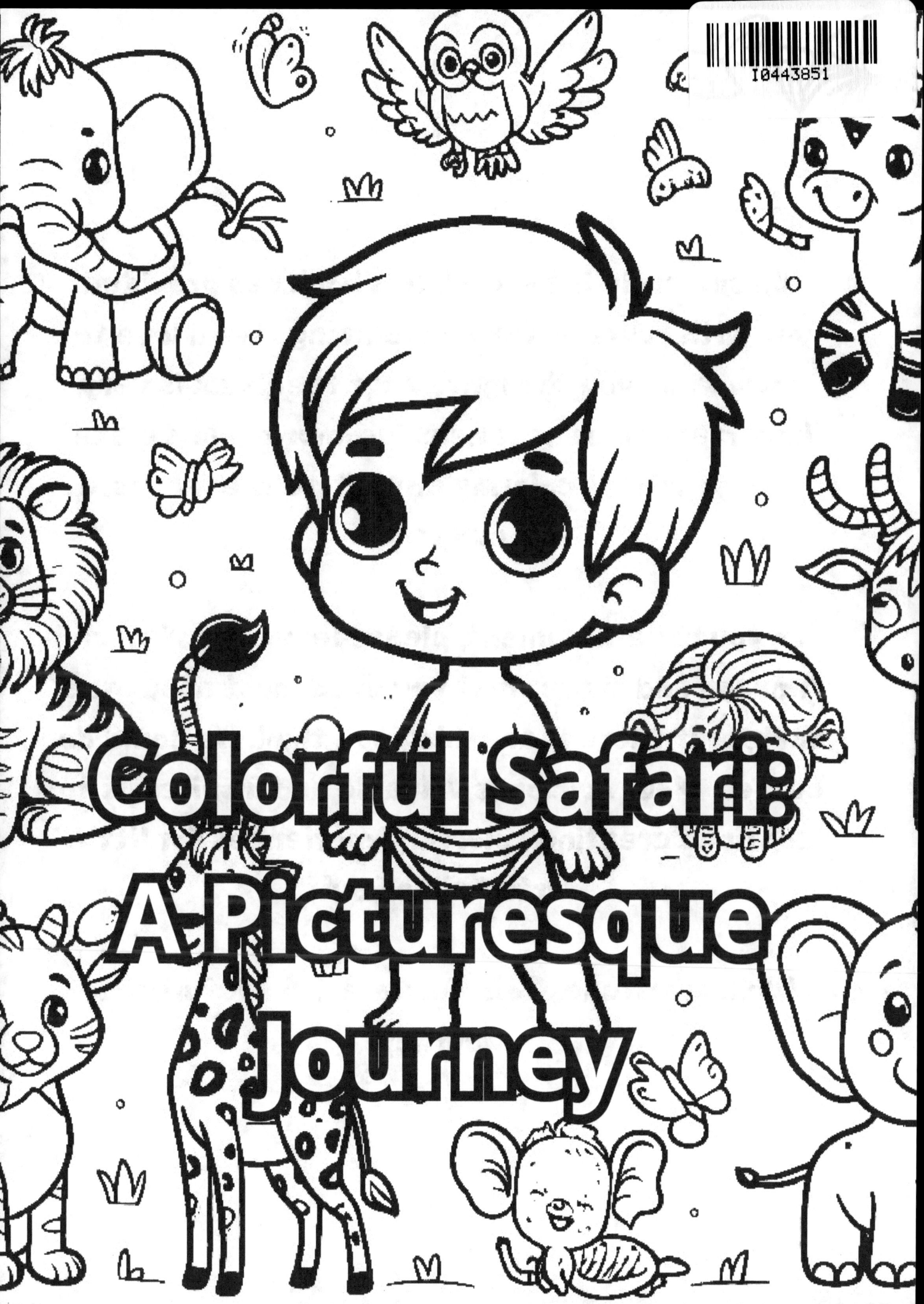

We sincerely hope that this book has provided you with hours of fun and learning. We'd love to know what you thought. Your feedback is very important to us as it helps us improve and make sure your next coloring adventure is even more magical.

If you have a moment, please leave a review on Amazon and share what you liked most about the book, or if there is anything you think we could do better. Your opinion is valuable and inspires us to continue creating colorful experiences for little artists like you!

With gratitude, Colorful Safari: A Picturesque Journey

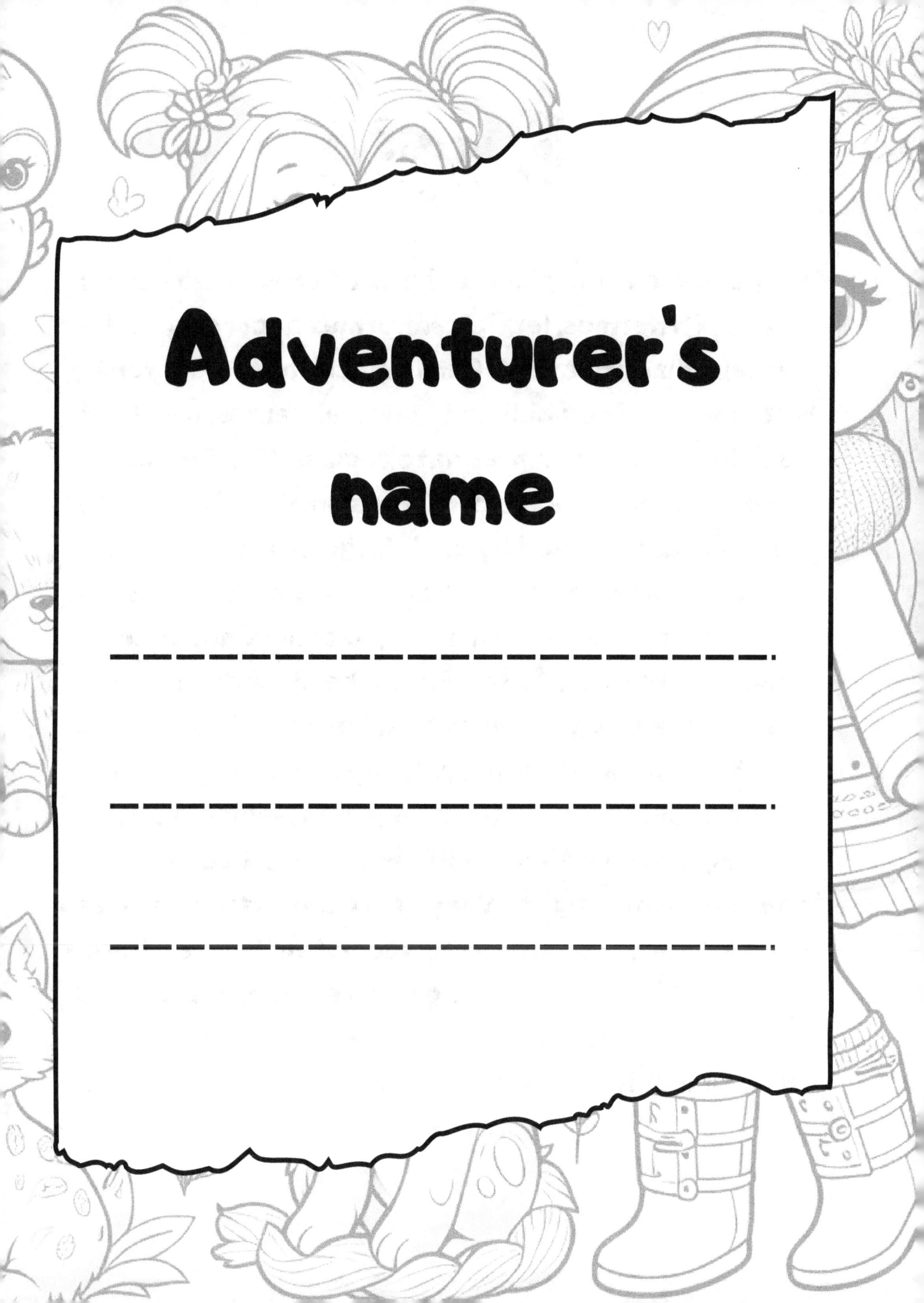
Adventurer's name

_____

_____

_____

Eagle

Eagle is the name given to birds of prey, of the order Accipitriformes, (or Falconiformes according to a previous classification), family Accipitridae, subfamily Buteoninae. They belong to several genres, which are subject to more appropriate reclassification since experts do not reach a consensus opinion. Eagles are mainly characterized by their large size, robust build, heavy head and beak. The various species and subspecies of eagles can be found almost anywhere in the world except Antarctica. Like all birds of prey, eagles have a large, powerful and pointed beak to tear off the flesh of their prey. They also have powerful claws and shanks. The strength of eagles is also striking, allowing them to lift prey much heavier than themselves into flight. They also have extremely sharp eyesight that allows them to see potential prey from a distance. For example, the golden eagle has two focal points in its eyes, one to look straight ahead and the other to locate its gaze to the sides, scanning into the distance.

Eagle

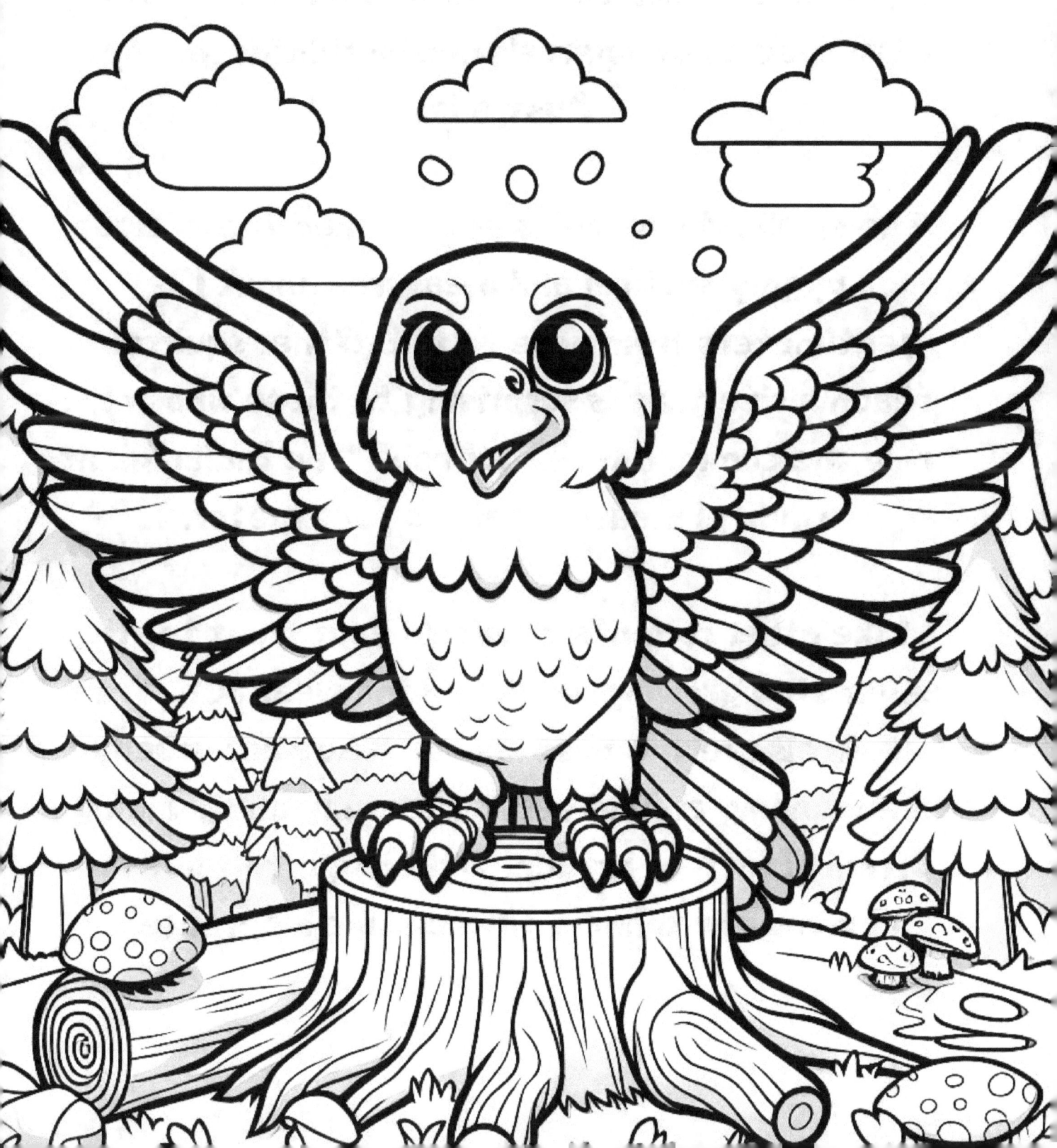

Squirrel

Squirrels are animals known to everyone. About 200 species of squirrels live worldwide, except Australia.

The smallest squirrel is aptly called the African pygmy squirrel and measures about 13 centimeters from nose to tail. Other squirrels reach a size that is surprising to those who only know the common tree squirrels. The Indian giant squirrel measures almost one meter.

Like other rodents, squirrels' four front teeth never stop growing, so they don't wear out. Tree squirrels are the best known. They are usually seen running around very gracefully and jumping from branch to branch. Other squirrels live in burrows or tunnels, where some hibernate.

Squirrel

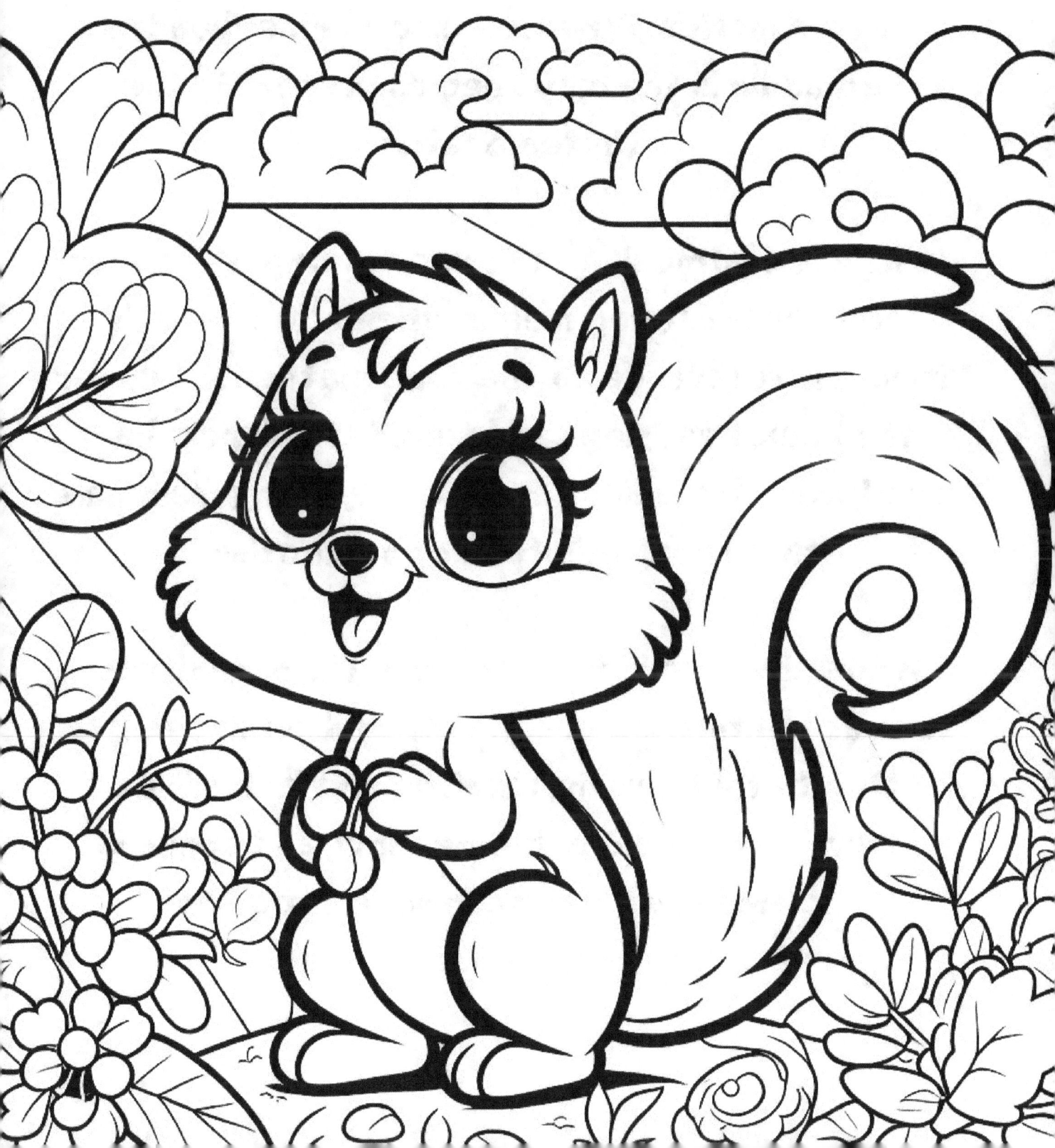

Armadillo

Of the 20 varieties of armadillo, all but one live in Latin America. The well-known nine-banded armadillo is the only species present in the United States.

The word "armadillo", also used in English, comes from Spanish, and means "the little one with armor", in reference to the bone plates that cover the back, head, legs and tail of these peculiar creatures. Armadillos are the only living mammals that sport this type of protection.

Armadillos live in temperate or warm habitats, such as rainforests, grasslands, and semi-deserts. Due to their low metabolism and lack of fat reserves, the cold is their enemy, and spells of inclement weather can wipe out entire populations.

Armadillo

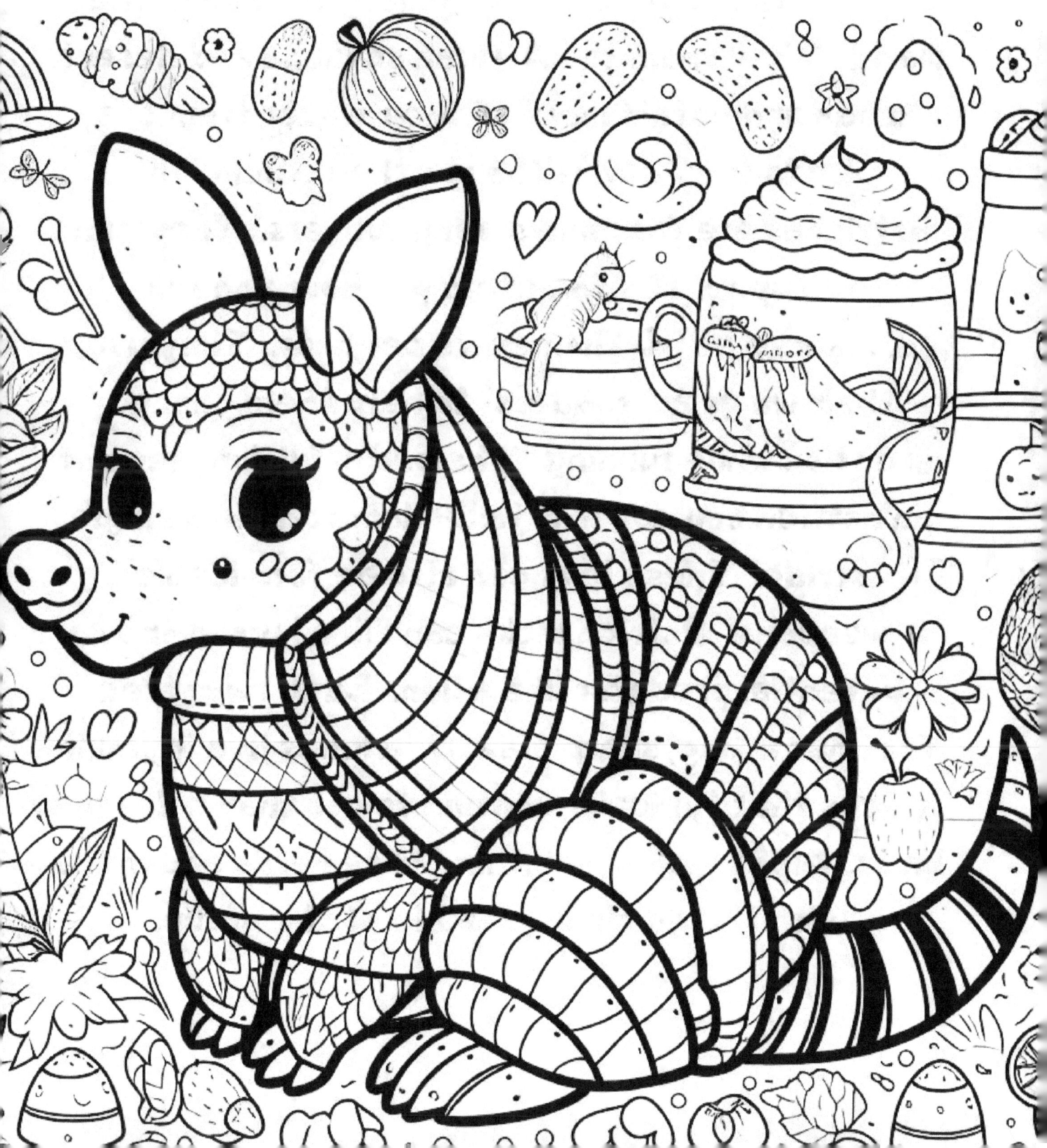

Ostrich

The flightless ostrich is the largest bird in the world. They roam the African savanna and desert lands and obtain most of their water from the plants they eat. Although they cannot fly, ostriches are fast and strong runners. They can run up to 70 kilometers per hour and run distances at 50 kilometers per hour. They use their wings as "rudders" to help them change direction while running. The powerful, long legs of an ostrich can cover 3 to 5 kilometers in a single stride. These legs can also be formidable weapons. Ostrich kicks can kill a human or a potential predator like a lion. Each two-toed foot has a long, sharp claw. Ostriches live in small flocks that typically contain fewer than a dozen birds. Alpha males maintain these herds and mate with the dominant female of the group.

Ostrich

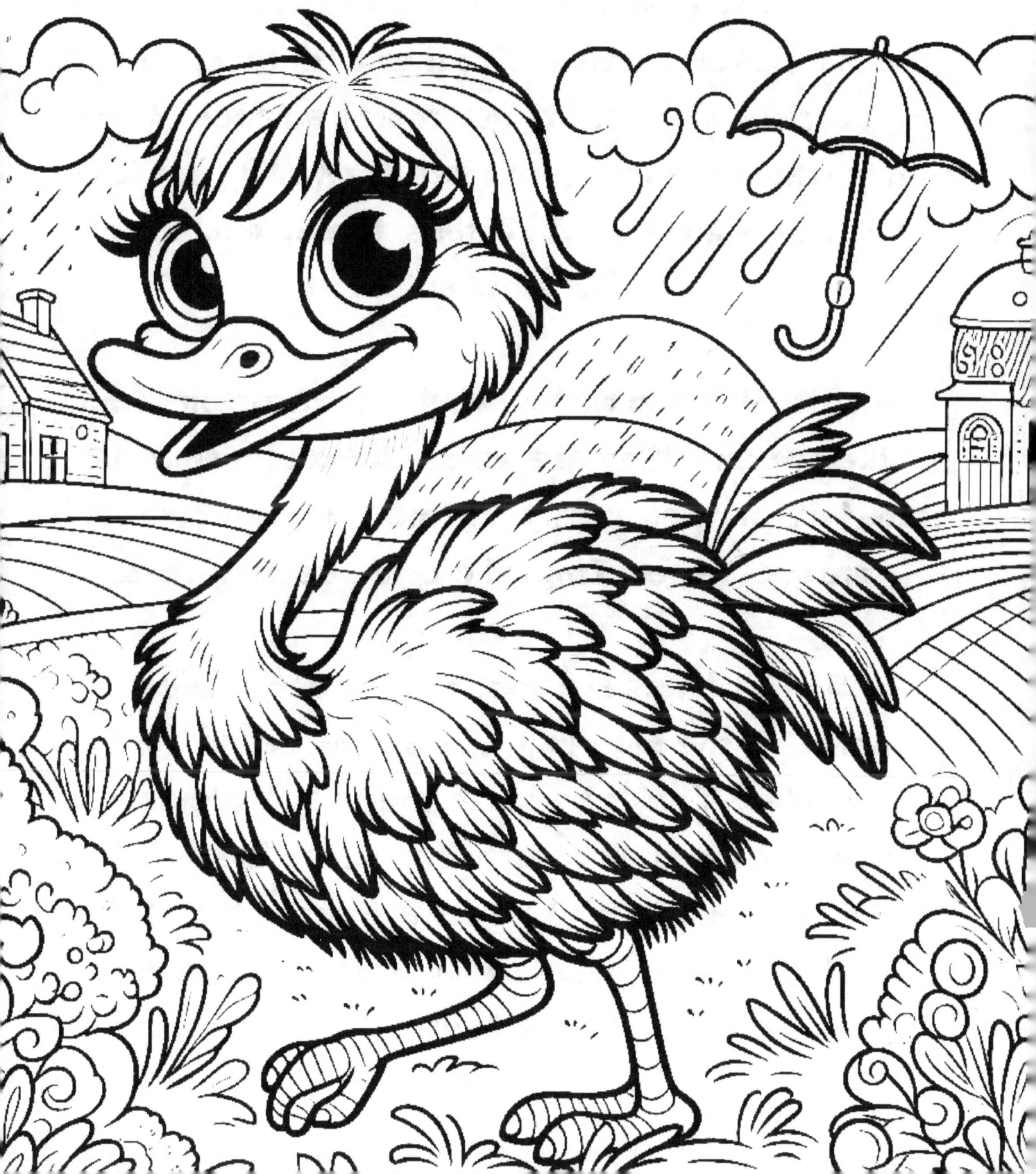

Whale

Whales navigate all the world's oceans, communicating with each other with complex and mysterious sounds. Its great size amazes us: the blue whale can measure more than 100 feet (30 m) and weigh up to 200 tons, the equivalent of 33 elephants.

Despite living in water, whales breathe air. And, like humans, they are warm-blooded mammals that nurse their young. A thick layer of blubber protects them from the cold ocean waters.

Some whales are known as baleen whales, including the blue, right, bowhead, sei and gray whales. This is because they have special structures in their mouth that resemble bristles (called baleen) that filter food from water. Other whales, such as beluga whales or sperm whales, have teeth.

Whale

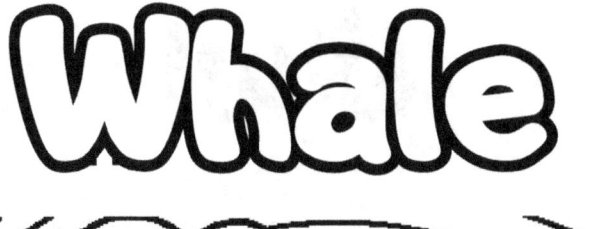

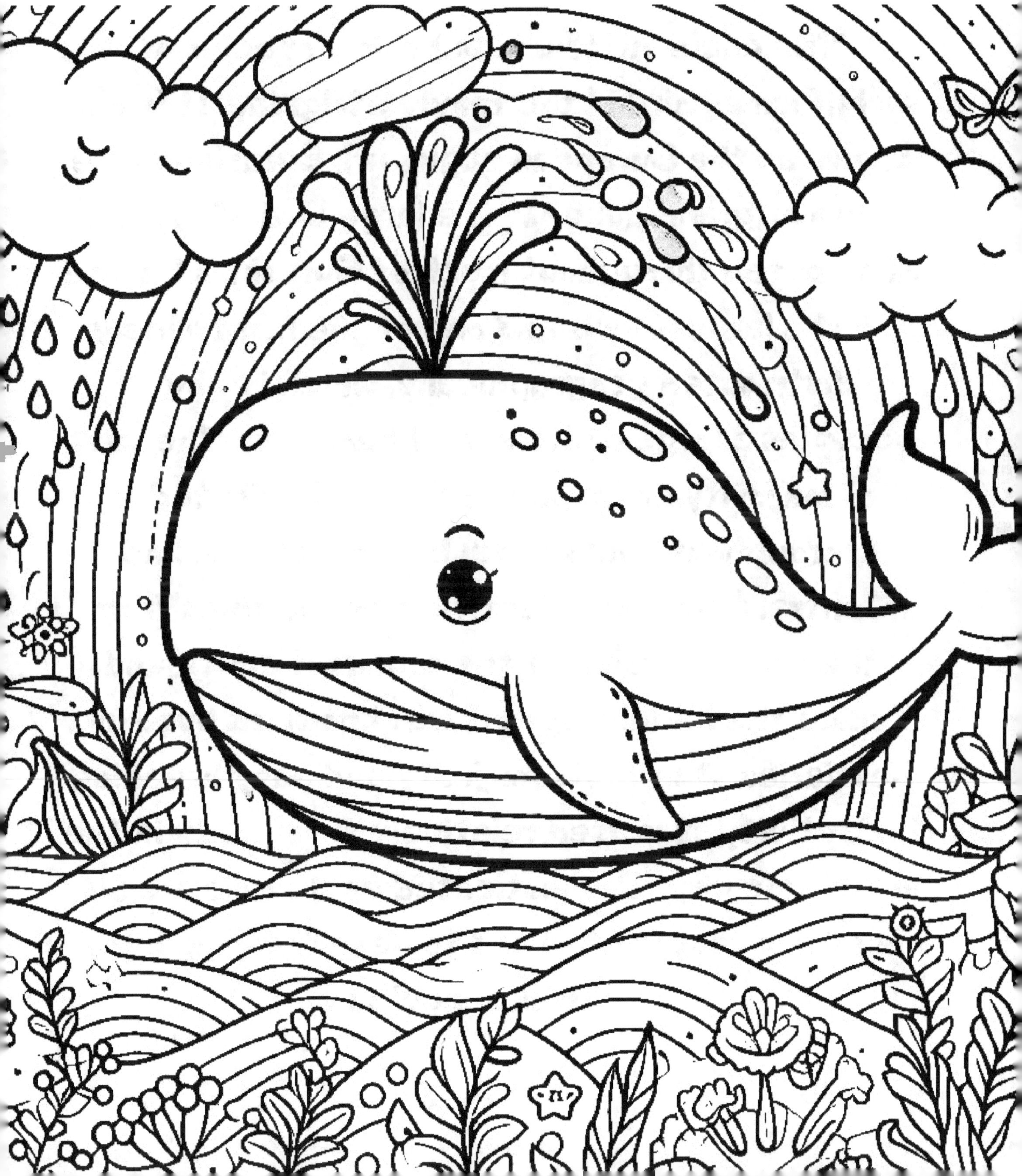

Owl

The eagle owl (Bubo bubo) is a species of strigiformes bird in the family Strigidae. It is also known as the European eagle owl, Eurasian eagle owl or grand duke. It is a large bird of prey, distributed throughout much of Eurasia. It is one of the largest owls and one of the most widely distributed geographically, which is why it occupies a large multitude of habitats. The vast majority of its population is distributed throughout continental Europe, Russia and Central Asia. Its scientific name derives from the onomatopoeia of the sounds it emits, and since the Middle Ages it was known as bubo in bestiaries. Due to its majesty and easy breeding in captivity, it is used relatively frequently in the art of falconry. Domesticated eagle owls are also used for pest control and to deter nesting birds such as seagulls.(

Owl

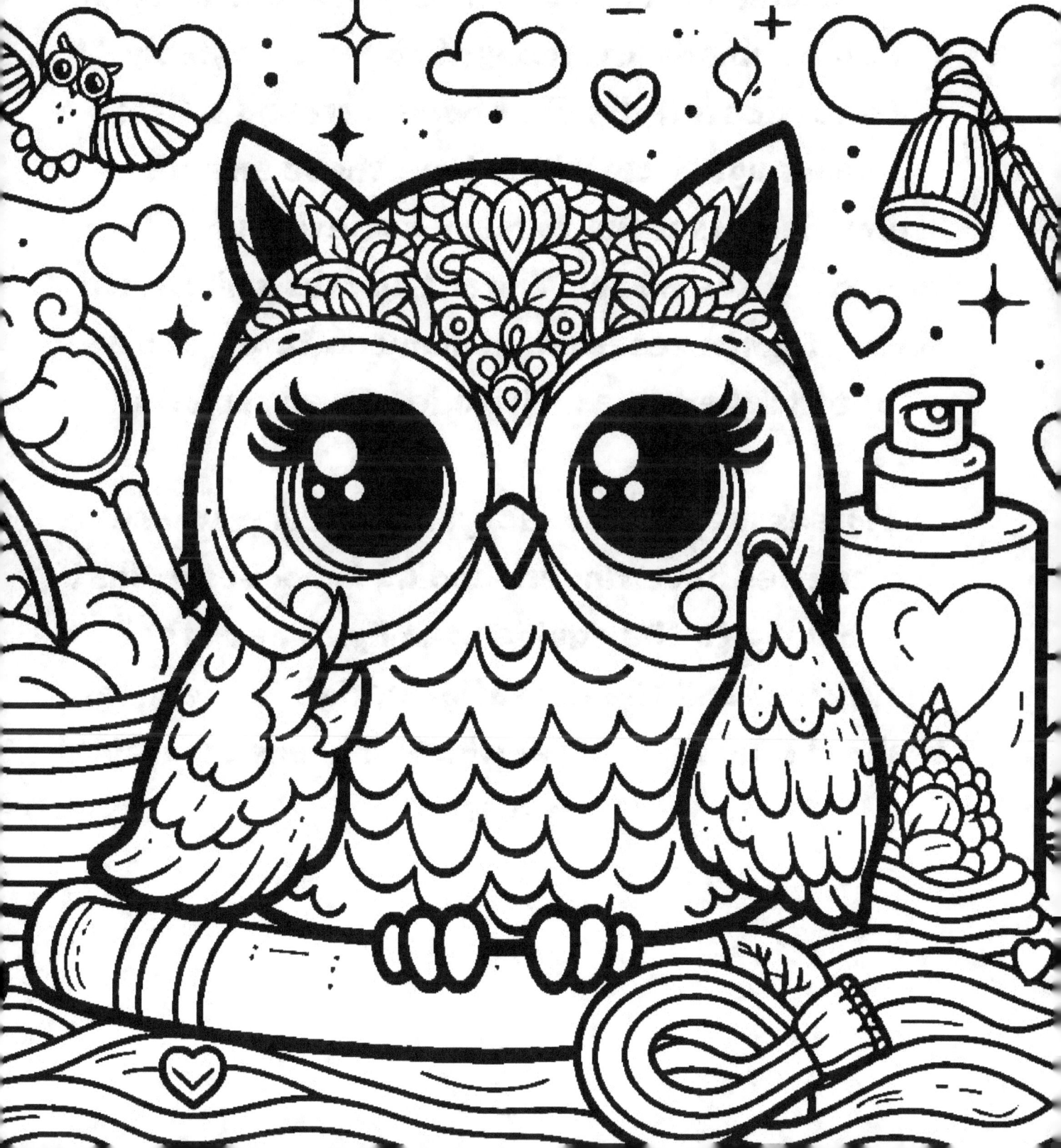

Horse

Horses and humans have a very old relationship. Asian nomads are thought to have probably domesticated the first horses around 4,000 years ago, from which time these animals remained essential to many societies until the advent of the motor. In fact, horses still have a place of honor reserved in many cultures, and are often linked to a multitude of war exploits.

Horses are perissodactyl mammals — whose extremities have fingers ending in hooves — that belong to the equidae family. They are herbivores and the gestation period for females is about 11 months, after which only one offspring is born.

Horse

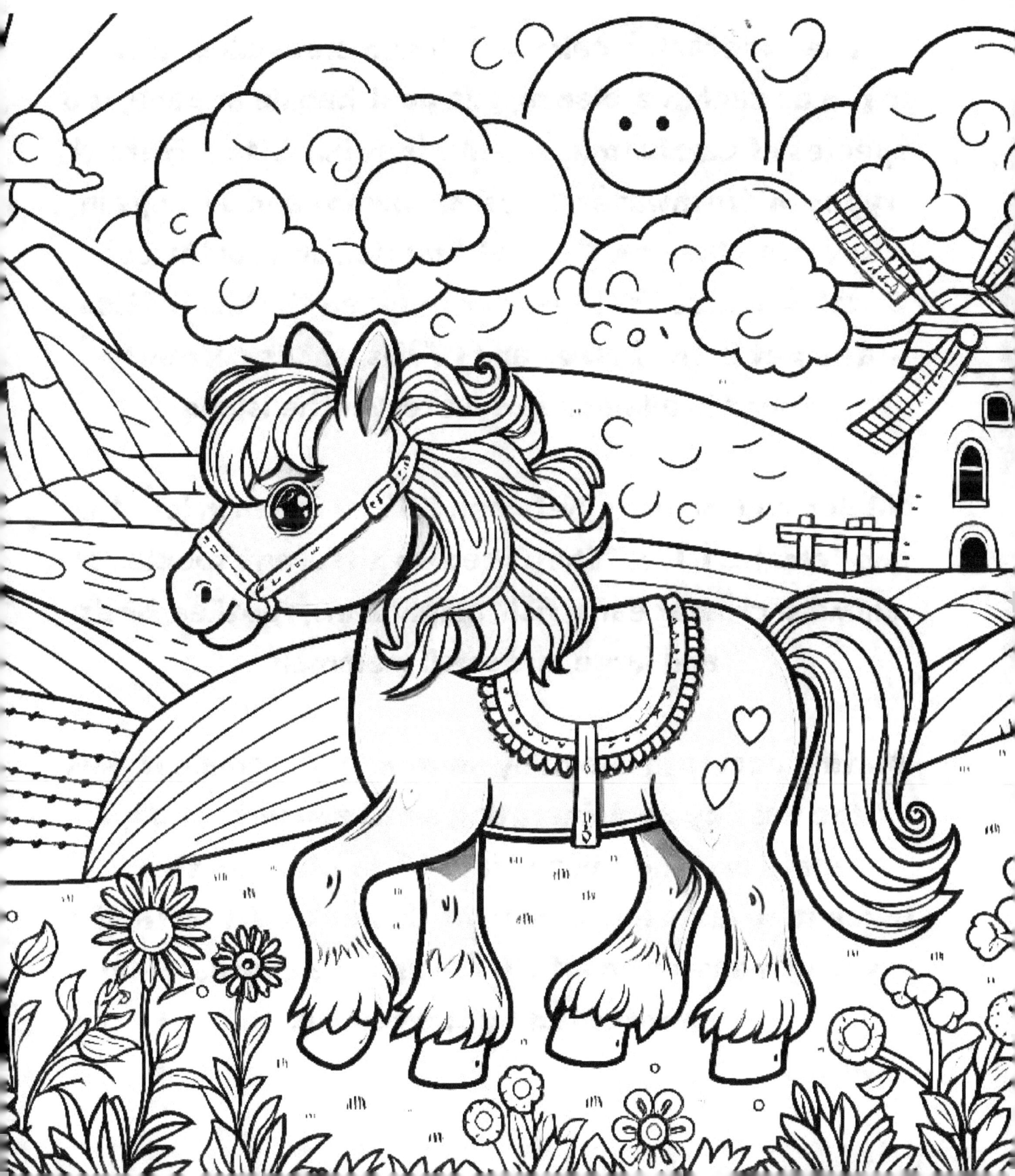

Alligator

The spectacled caiman (Caiman crocodilus), also known as cachirre, blanco, guagipal, babilla or baba, is a species of carnivorous reptile that inhabits different types of freshwater courses, swamps and swamps in southern Mexico, Central America and northwest South America.(3) It was introduced to Puerto Rico as a pet in the 1960s and 1970s, and is currently found in all bodies of water on the island.

Males can measure between 1.8 and 2.5 m in length, and females 1.4m. They feed on different species of animals: crustaceans, fish, amphibians, reptiles, birds and large and small mammals.

Mating occurs in the rainy season. The female makes the nest by agglomerating small amounts of dry vegetation and soil and lays 15 to 40 eggs there. Incubation lasts an average of 13 weeks. At birth, the young measure about 20 cm and are aggressively protected by the female.

Alligator

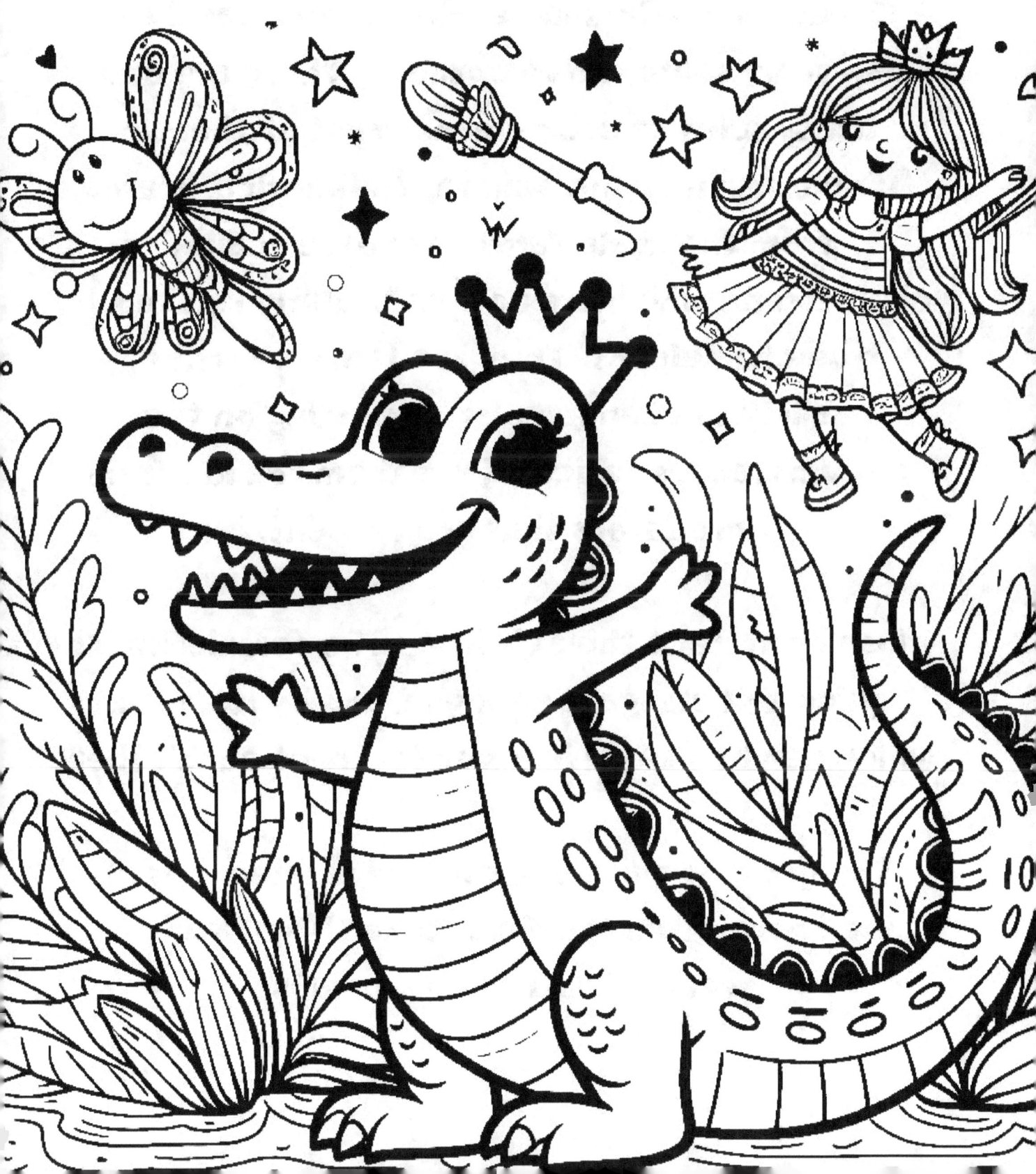

Chameleon

Chameleons (Chamaeleonidae) are a family of small scaly sauropsids (reptiles). There are about 161 species of chameleons, most of them in Africa, south of the Sahara. In America, lizards from the anole family are often called chameleons, which are not particularly related to true chameleons. They are famous for their ability to change color depending on the circumstances, which allows them to hide from predators that are present.

close or attract the attention of a female, by its quick and elongated tongue, and by its eyes, which can be moved independently of each other.

The group is quite old, since chameleon fossils are known from the Paleocene. The family is related with the agámidos.

Chameleon

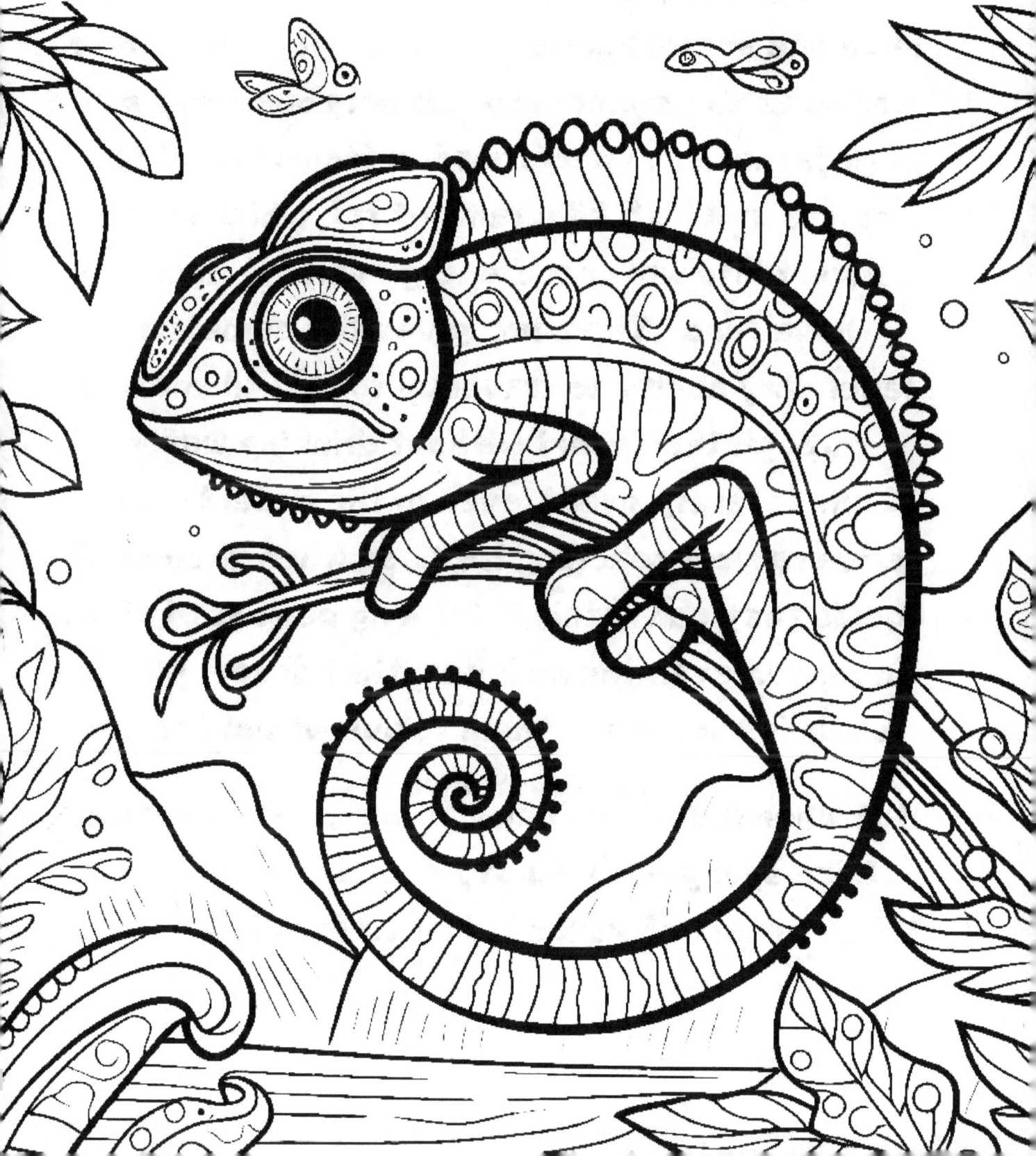

Camel

The typical question about camels is: do they have one or two humps? The Arabian camel, also known as the dromedary, has only one hump but gets maximum performance from it. In it it stores up to 36 kilograms of fat, which it can convert into water and energy when it does not have food. The hump gives the camel its legendary ability to travel up to 160 kilometers through the desert without drinking water. Camels rarely sweat, even in the desert under temperatures reaching 49°C, so when they drink liquids they can retain it for long periods of time. In winter, even the moisture that desert plants retain is enough for them to live without water for several weeks.
But when camels refuel with water, they soak up it like sponges. A thirsty camel can drink 135 liters of water in just 13 minutes.

Camel

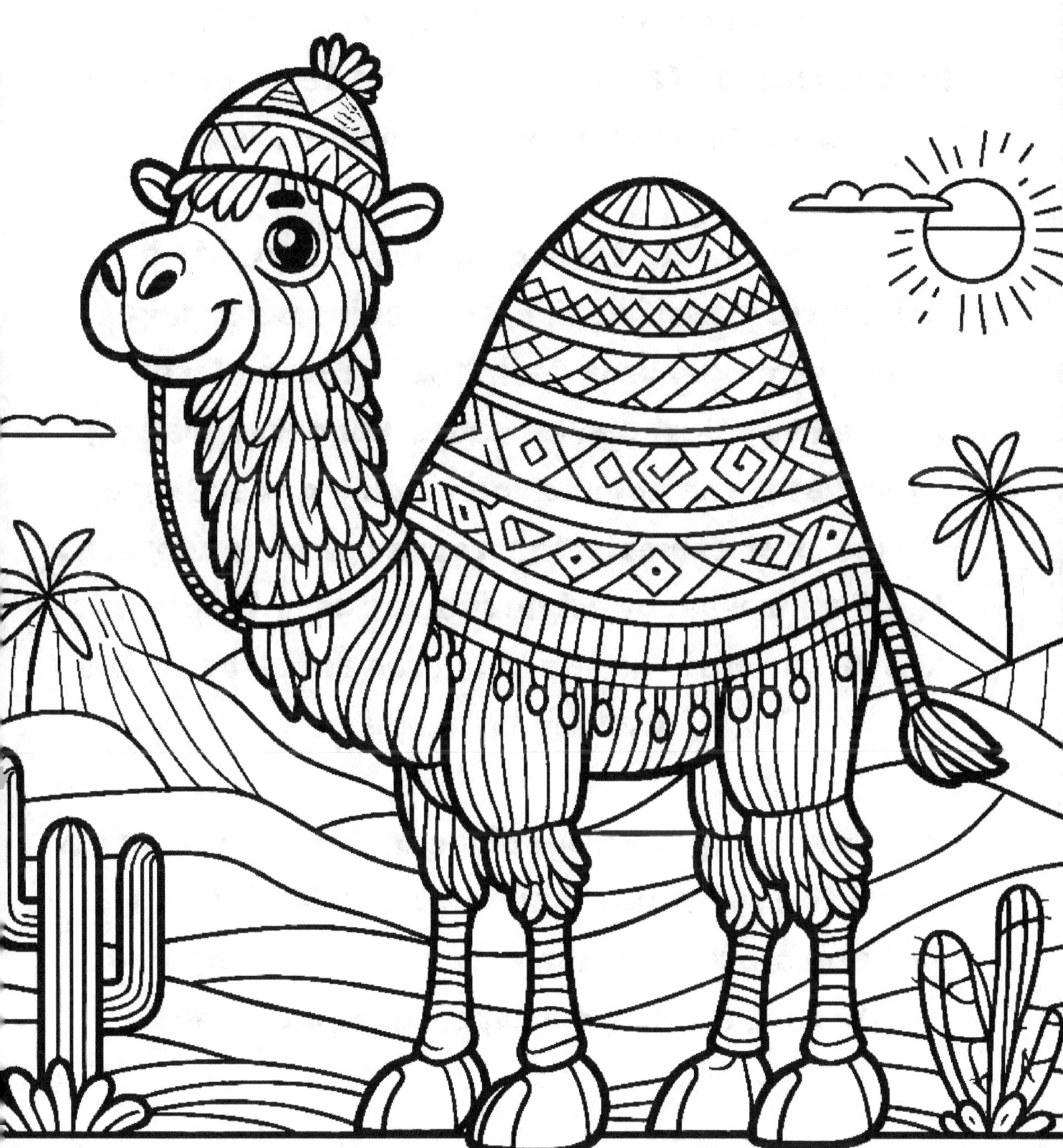

Kangaroo

The term kangaroo is the common name used to designate the largest species of the Macropodidae family, just as the term wallaby is used to designate the smaller ones.

However, the term does not respond to a scientific classification, so species belonging to the same genus (a term that groups closely related species) can be called kangaroo, wallaby or wallaby, the common name only depending on its size. For example, Macropus parma is known as the Parma wallaby, while Macropus antilopinus is known variously as the kangaroo antelope or the wallaby antelope.

The subfamily Macropodinae includes, in addition to the species of kangaroos, wallabies and wallabies, others commonly known as kangaroos. arboreal, cuocas, dorcopsis and pademelons.

Kangaroo

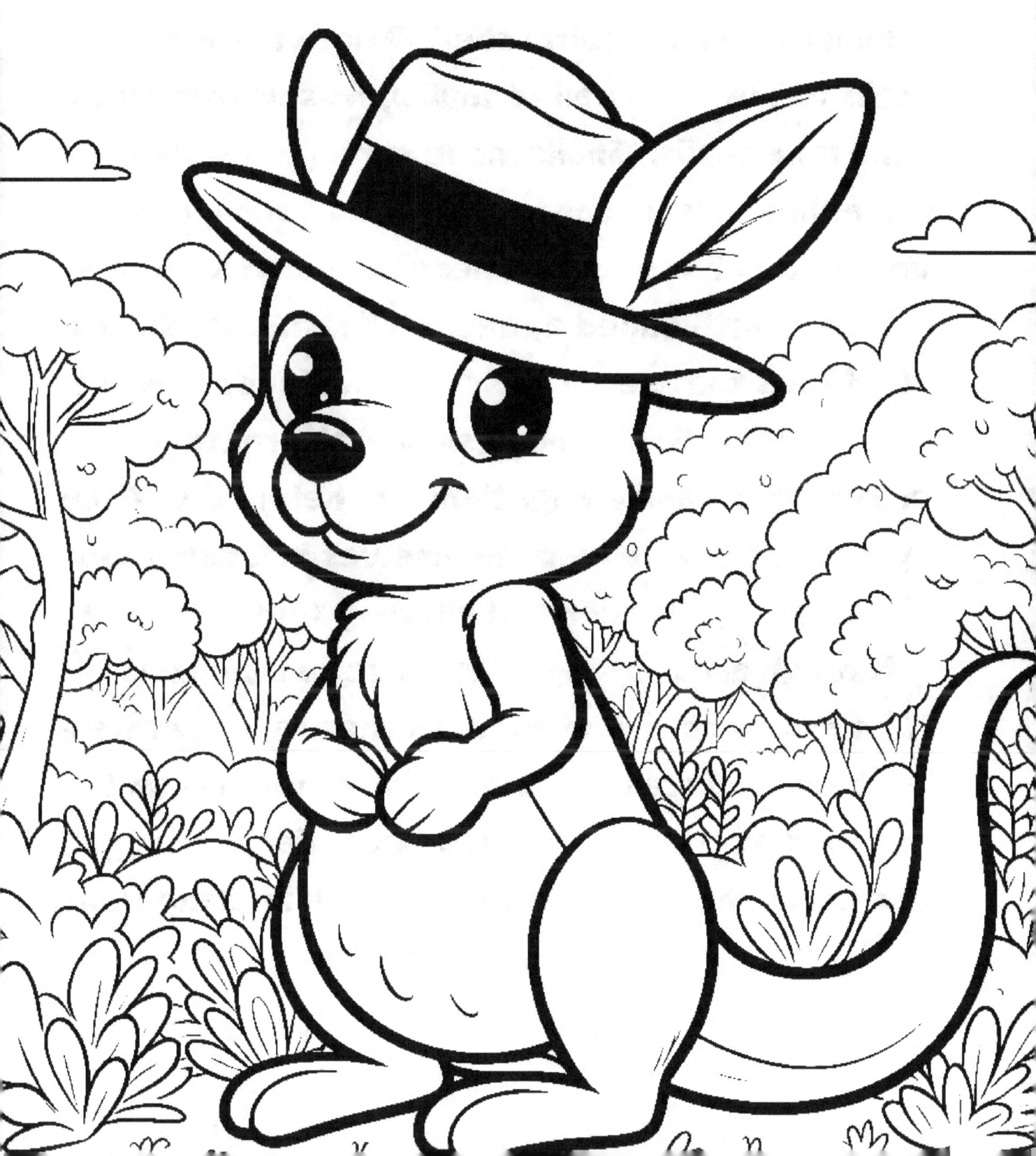

Snail

The term snail is the common name for gastropod mollusks with a spiral shell. There are marine snails (sometimes called snails), freshwater snails, and land snails. Snails move through a series of wave-like muscle contractions that run along the underside of the foot. These have a structure in their mouth called a radula, with thousands of denticles that serve to scrape surfaces in order to feed. Snails move slowly, alternating contractions and elongations of their body. They produce slime to help themselves in locomotion by reducing friction and allowing them to move through areas of high slope due to its oiliness. This mucus contributes to its thermal regulation; It also reduces the snail's risk of wounds and external aggressions, mainly bacterial and fungal, and helps them scare away potentially dangerous insects such as ants.

Snail

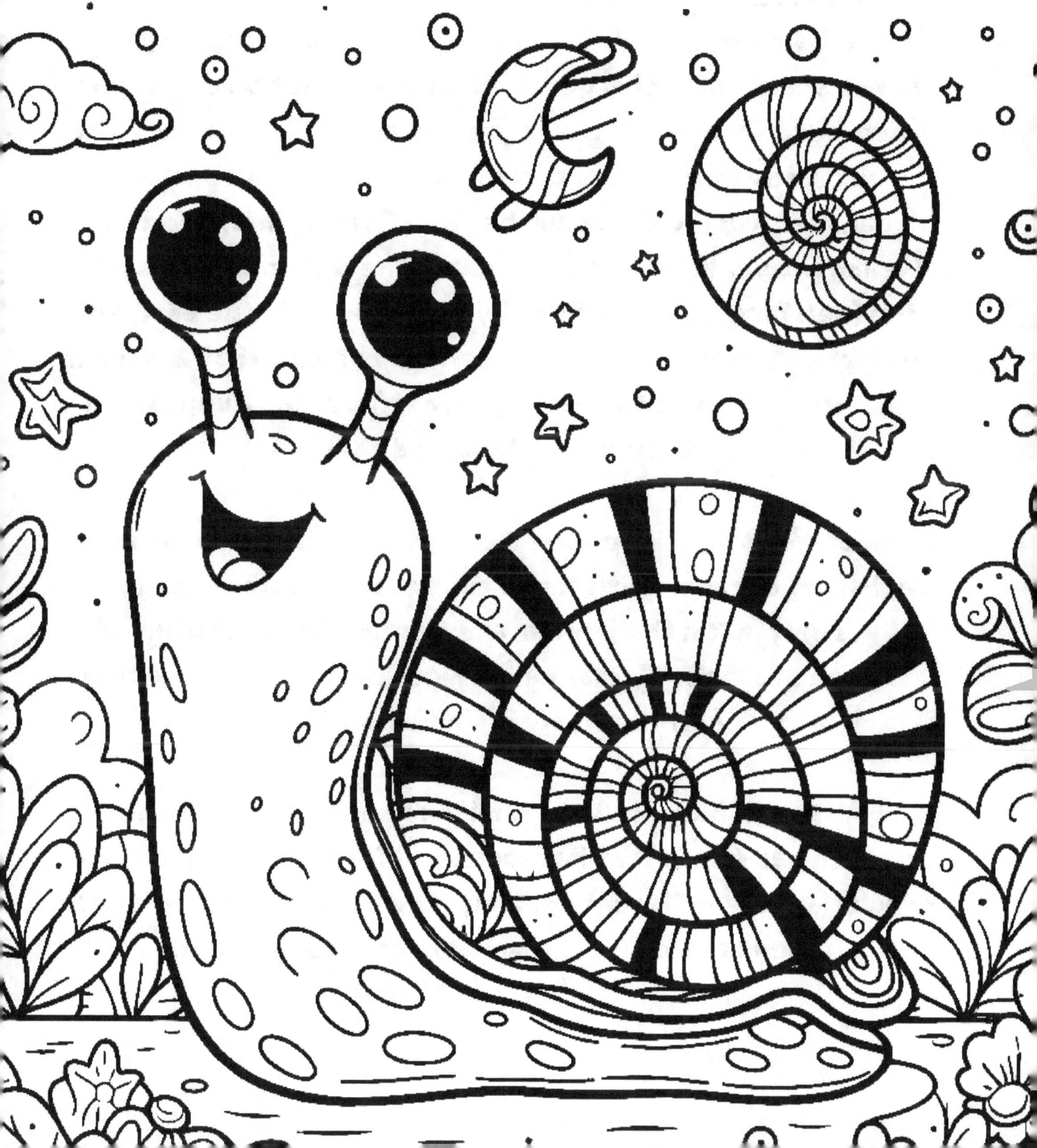

Beaver

Beavers (Castor) are a genus of semi-aquatic rodents native to North America and Eurasia that are characterized by their broad, scaly tails. This genus, of all those that belong to the Castoridae family, is the only one not completely extinct, and includes three species: the American beaver (Castor canadensis), the European beaver (Castor fiber) and the Kellog beaver (Castor californicus), the latter extinct since the Pleistocene. All of them live exclusively in the northern hemisphere, except for some American beavers that arrived in the Argentine and Chilean region of Tierra del Fuego when they were introduced there.

Specimens of this species were also introduced in certain regions of Europe. With these exceptions, Castor canadensis lives only in North America, and Castor fiber in regions of Europe and Asia. Castor californicus ranged across what is now the western United States.

Although they are very similar to each other, genetic research has shown that European and North American beaver populations are different species; The main difference is that they have different numbers of chromosomes.

Beaver

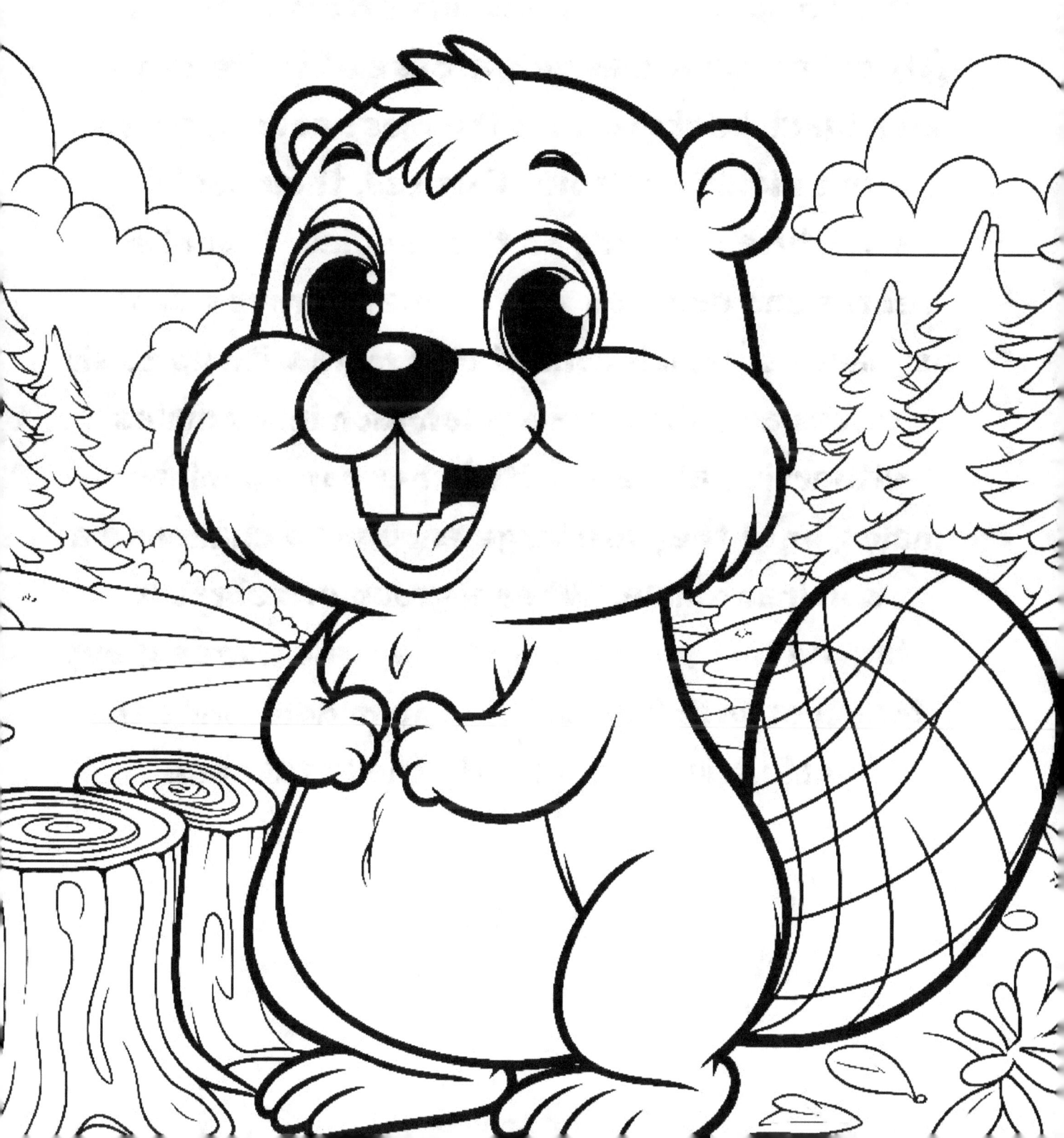

Zebra

Three species of the genus Equus, native to Africa, are known as zebra. base of white stripes on a black background. Like most equids, zebras are highly sociable. Even so, their social structure depends on the species. Mountain zebras and common zebras live in groups, known as "harems," which consist of a male with up to six mares and their foals. Non-dominant males either live alone or with other non-dominant males, until they are large enough to challenge a dominant male. When a group of zebras is attacked by hyenas or wild dogs, the mares group together with the foals in the middle while the male tries to scare off the attackers.

Zebra

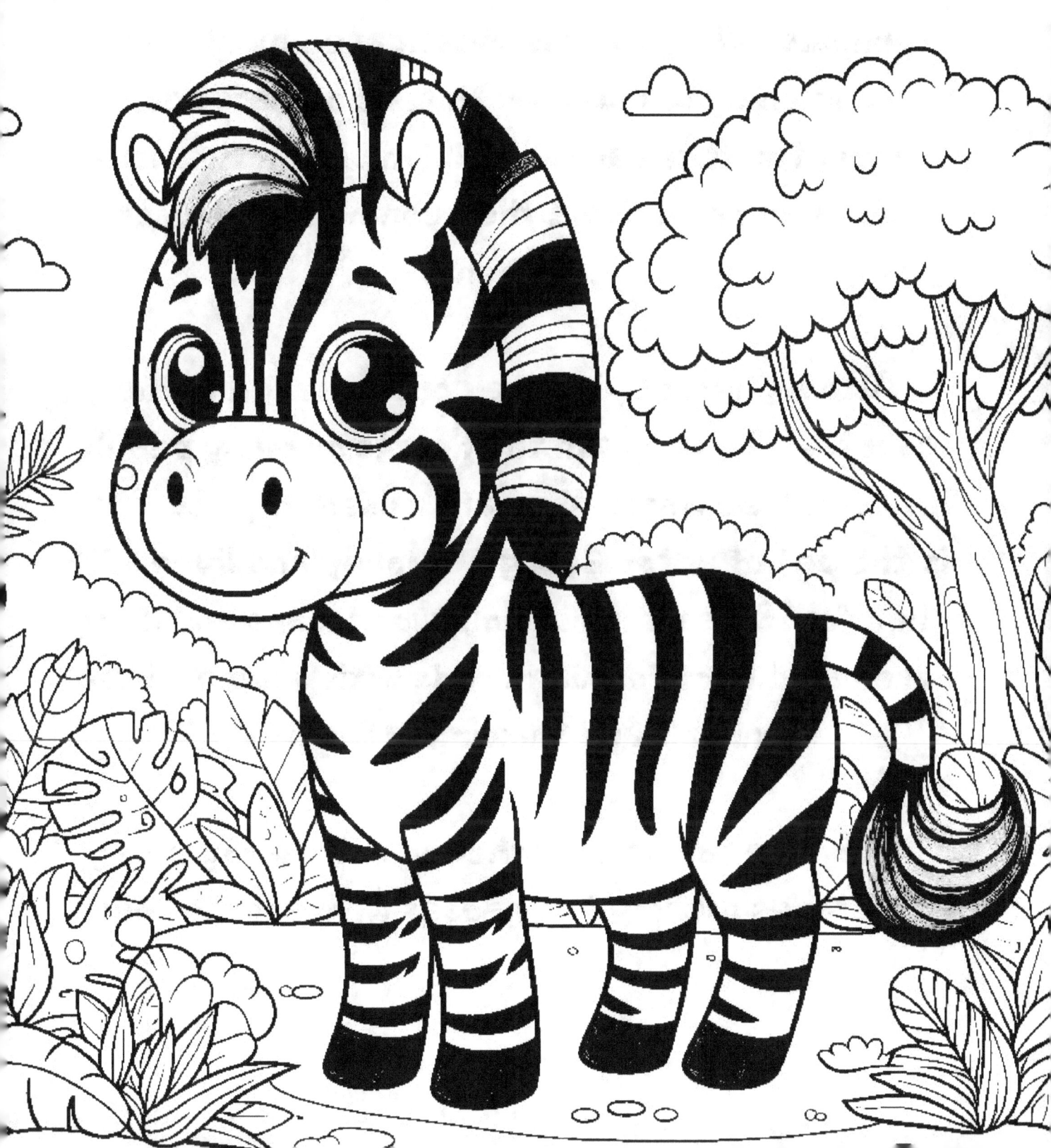

Pig

Pigs are one of the oldest species of farm animals. They were domesticated by humans, even before cows, six thousand years ago. Currently, there are one billion pigs in the world (approximately) and they can be found on all continents.

Although most pigs are concentrated in the countryside, they win the hearts of many people in the cities, where they are raised as pets. Max is the pet of actor George Clooney and lived with him for 18 years in his Hollywood mansion. They are capable of forming bonds with people, other animals and showing affection.

They like to live together and sleep together, sometimes rubbing their noses with another pig's.

Pig

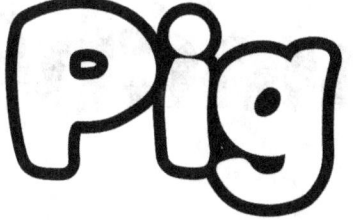

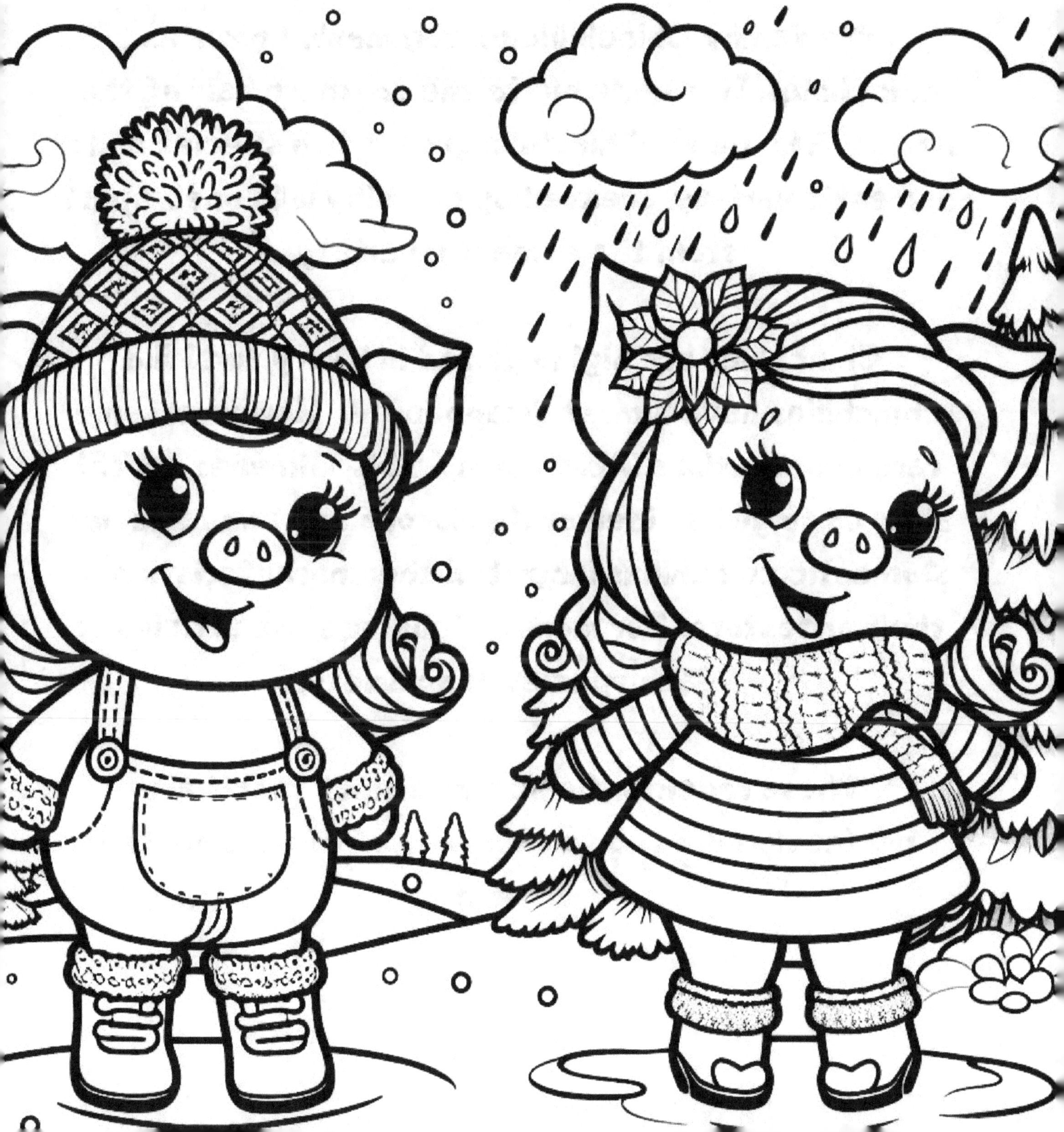

Chinchilla

Chinchilla is a genus of hystricomorphic rodents of the family Chinchillidae, commonly known as chinchillas. It is endemic to the southern half of the Andes. The genus Chinchilla groups two species and a domestic variety, created by crossing wild ones, apart from the domestic variety.

Chinchillas are highly prized in luxury fur. Wild chinchillas have almost disappeared. However, some rare observations (AE Brehm, 1864; Jiménez, 1995) allow us to get an idea of its morphology and behavior. Domestic chinchillas inherited the characteristics of their ancestors. For more details, see the articles on each species and variety.

These rodents the size of a small rabbit are perfectly adapted to their way of life in a hostile habitat.

Chinchilla

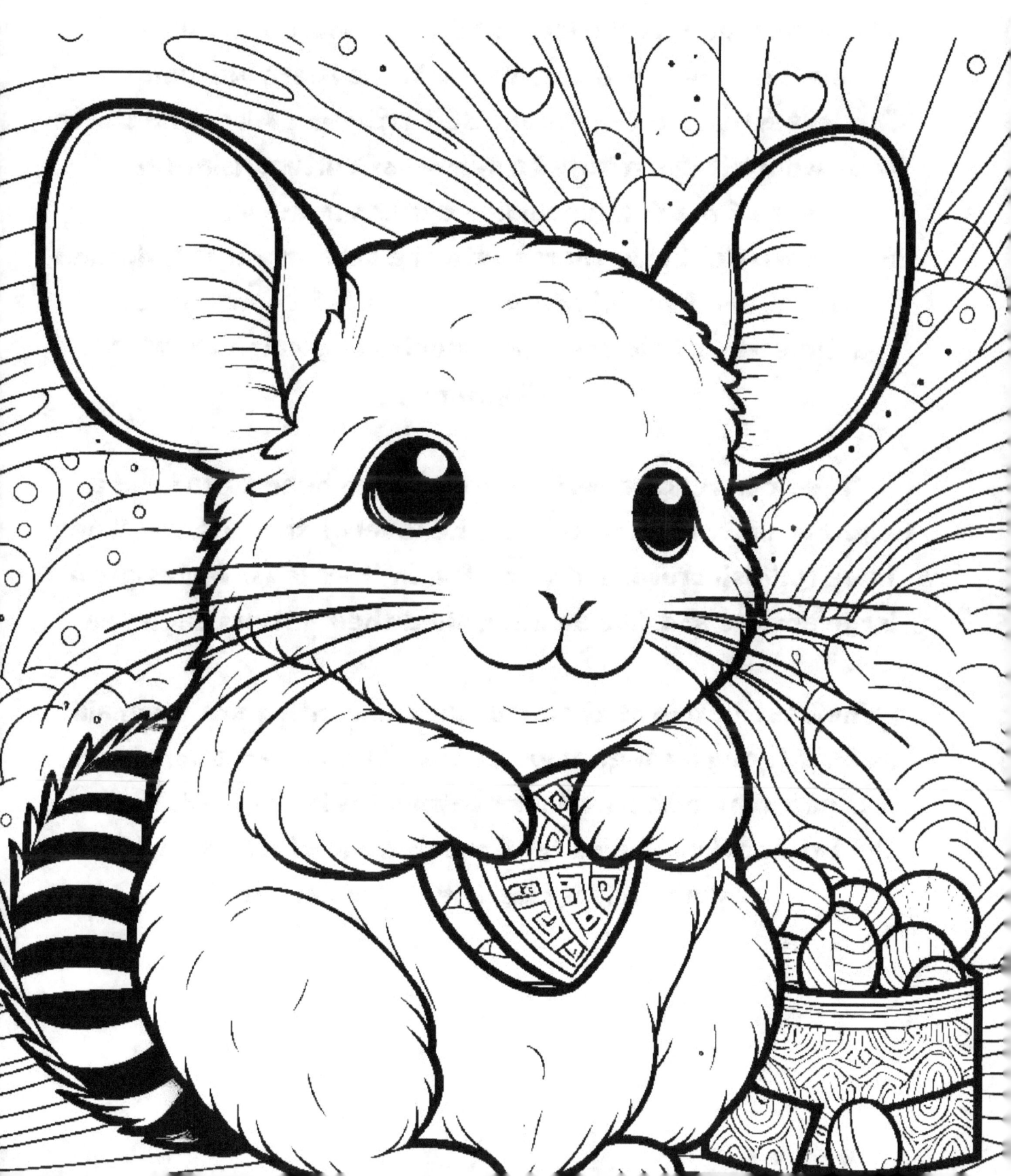

Deer

The swamp deer is the largest deer in South America and in our country it is found mainly in the Iberá Wetlands (Corrientes), and in the Paraná delta (Buenos Aires and Entre Ríos), where it constitutes a symbol of culture. islander It is one of the few amphibian cervids in the world, a characteristic it only shares with the barasingha of India and Nepal, and the water deer of China, which makes it a particularly unique specimen. Adults can weigh about 150 kilograms.

They can reach about 2 meters from head to tail and a height of up to 1.30 meters at the level of the withers. They have reddish brown and black fur on their legs. Males grow large antlers and, like all deer, shed their antlers each year.

The destruction of their habitat and hunting are the main threats faced by their populations. At an international level it is categorized as a vulnerable species in the Red Book of the International Union for Conservation of Nature, while in Argentina it is classified as endangered.

Deer

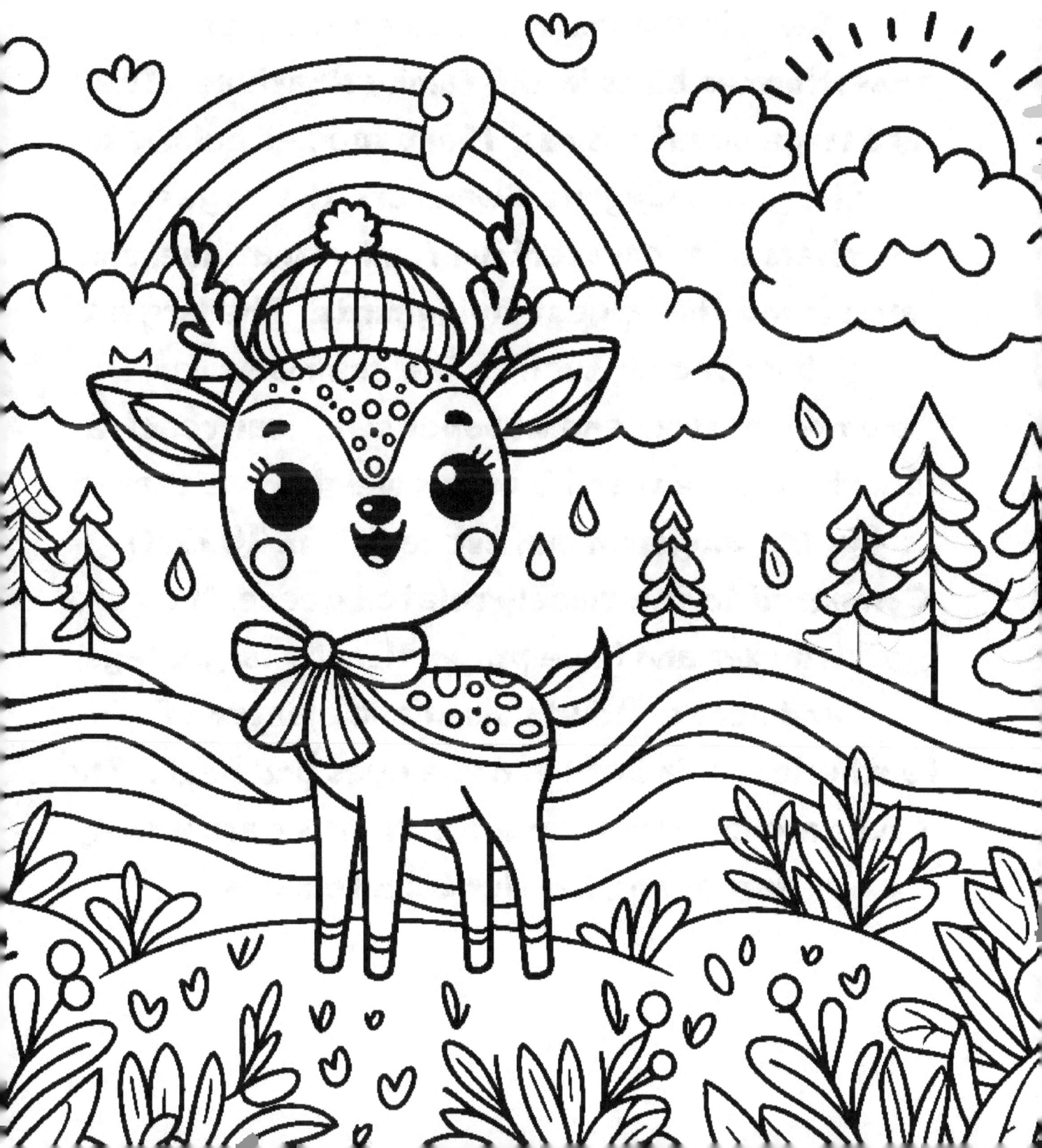

Swan

Swan is the common name for several anseriformes birds in the family Anatidae. They are large aquatic birds. Most species belong to the genus Cygnus. Swans are the largest members of the waterfowl family Anatidae, and are among the largest flying birds. The largest living species, such as the common swan, trumpeter swan and whooper swan, can reach a length of more than 1.5 m and weigh more than 15 kg. Its wingspan can exceed 3.1 m (10.2 ft). Compared to the closely related geese, they are much larger and have proportionally larger legs and necks. Adults also have a patch of featherless skin between the eyes and beak. The sexes are equal in plumage, but males are usually larger and heavier than females.

Swan

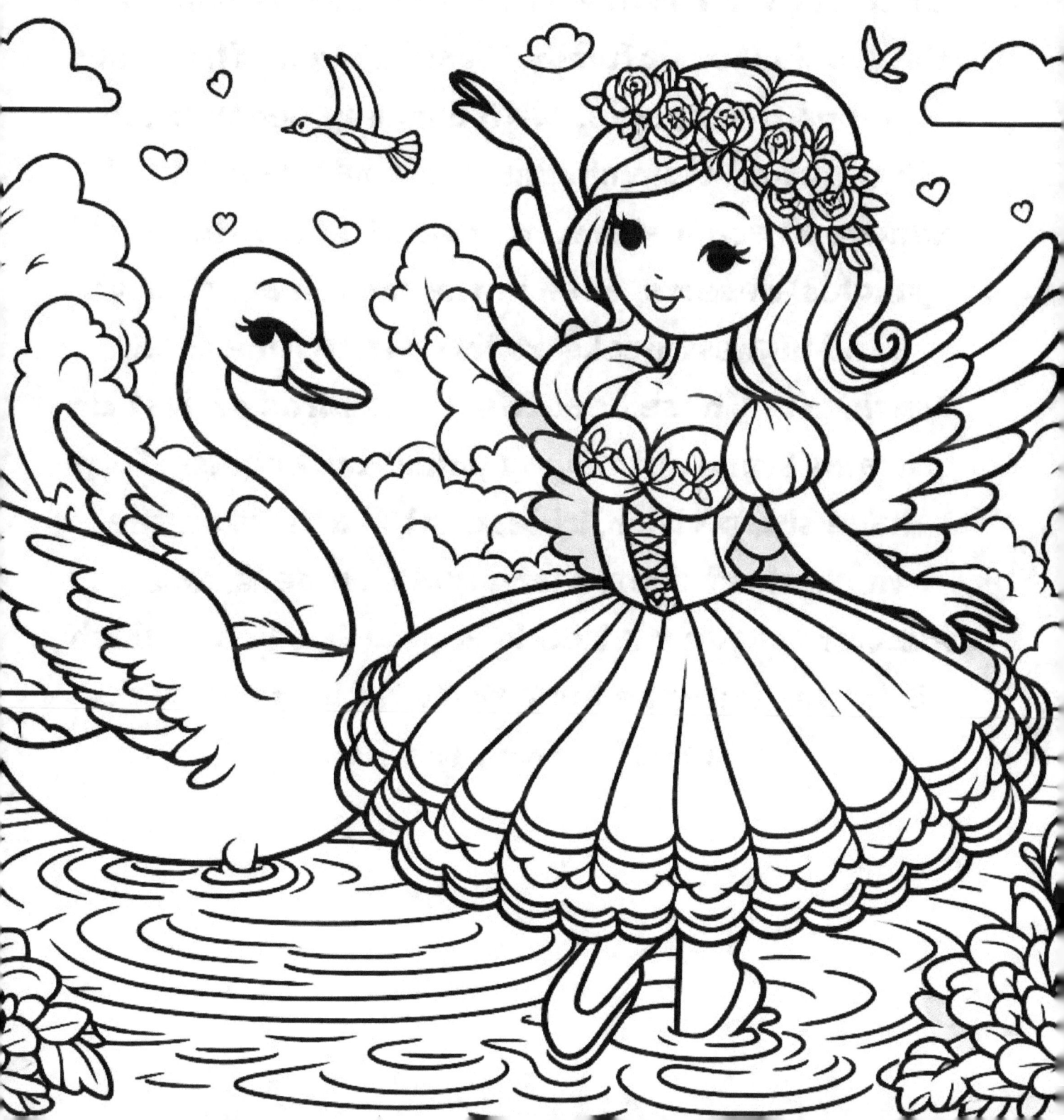

hummingbird

Colibri is a genus of apodiform birds belonging to the trochiline subfamily (Trochilinae). The genus groups five species with a mainly neotropical distribution. Hummingbirds are native beings to almost all ecosystems, temperate forests, humid jungles, deserts, even in the most mountainous and highest peaks of the entire American continent. These beautiful little birds of just 2-4 grams stand out among pollinator beings; They have sharp vision, iridescent feathers on the neck, short feet, a long and thin beak, and a tubular tongue that curls around the head, which is longer than the beak and with which it sucks the nectar from the flowers.

hummingbird

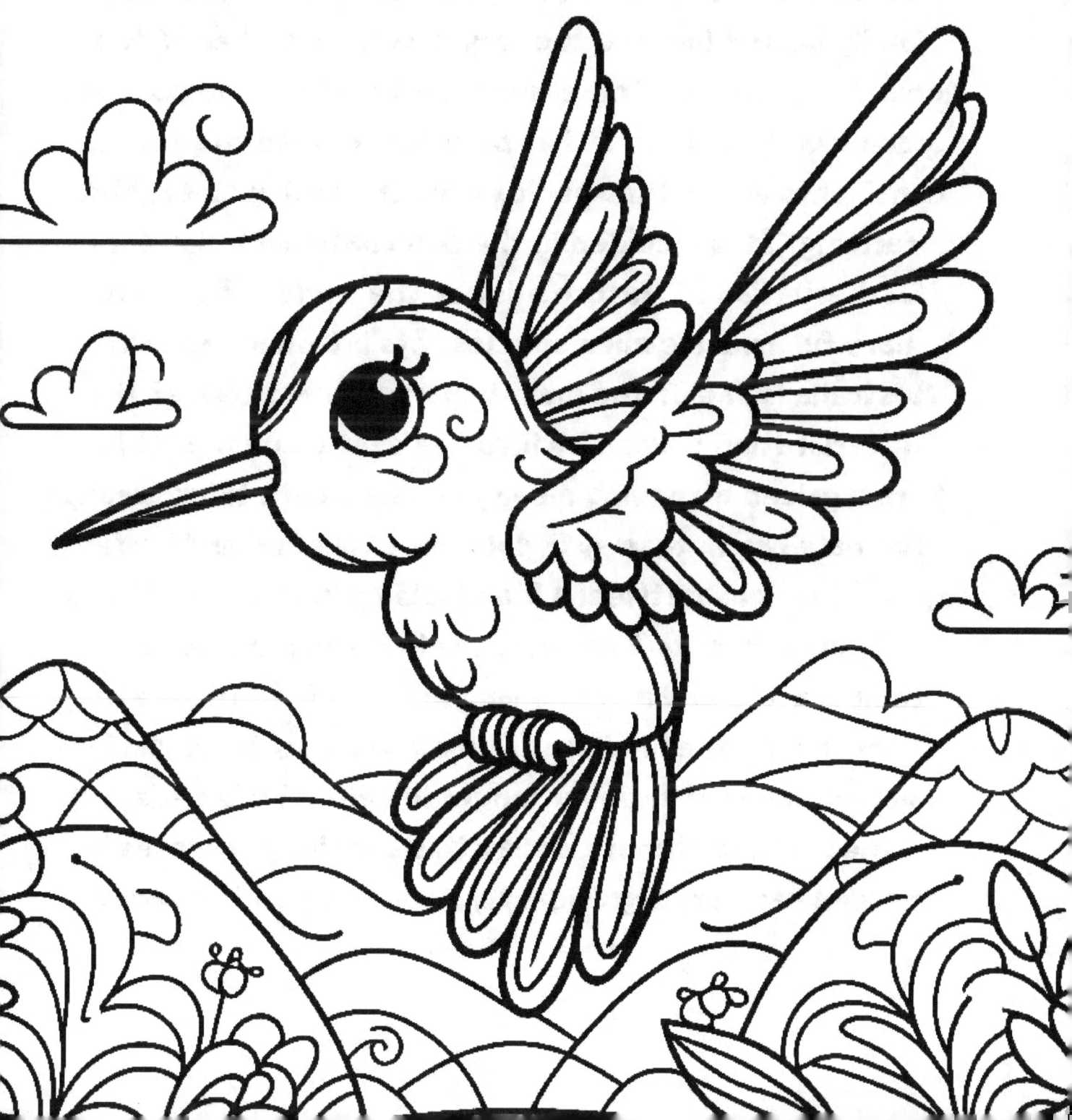

rabbit

The common rabbit or European rabbit (Oryctolagus cuniculus) is a species of lagomorphic mammal in the family Leporidae, and the only current member of the genus Oryctolagus. It measures up to 50 cm and its mass can be up to 2.5 kg. It has been introduced to several continents and is the species used in cooking and rabbit farming. It is included in the International Union for Conservation of Nature's list of the world's 100 most harmful invasive alien species. Its introduction into Australia is one of the most important chapters of the deterioration caused by invasive exotic species. It is characterized by having a body covered with thick, woolly fur, pale brown to gray in color, an oval head and large eyes. It weighs between 1.5 and 2.5 kg in the wild. It has long ears up to 7 cm which help it regulate body temperature and a very short tail. Their forelegs are shorter than the hindlegs. It measures 34 to 50 cm in favorable conditions, even longer in domestic breeds. All of these characteristics that this species possesses in the wild can vary significantly depending on the breed.

rabbit

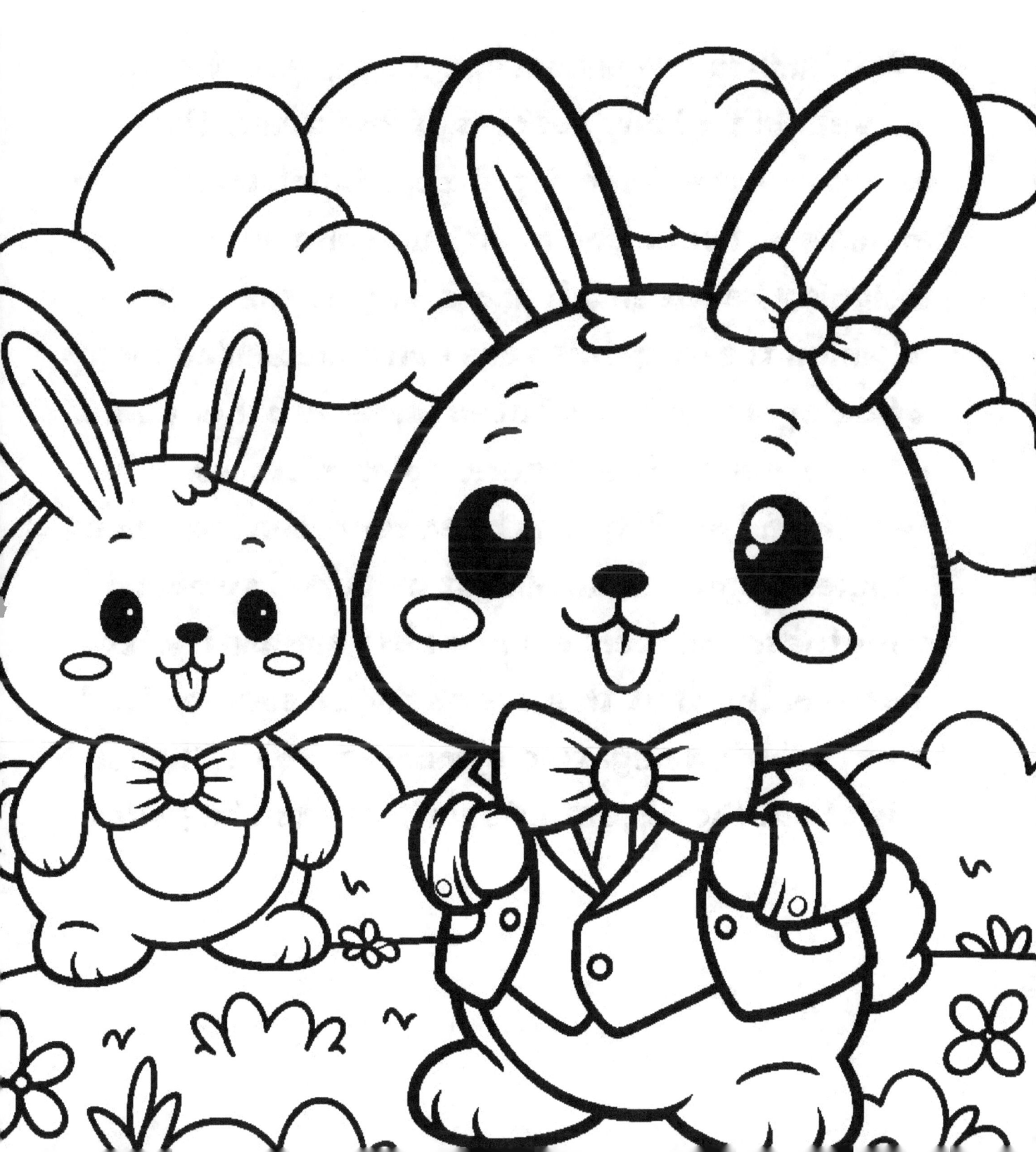

Lamb

The lamb is the animal specimen, less than one year old, of any species of the genus Ovis, especially the domestic sheep; Lamb meat, from animals between one month and one year old and weighing between 5.5 and 25 kg, is the main way in which these species are consumed. The meat of older sheep is marketed under another name. Lamb, due to the generic color of its wool, its youth and docility, has been represented since ancient times as an almost universal symbol of sweetness, innocence, meekness and purity. It is noteworthy that there is no known society that has attributed negative symbolism to it. The lamb is often the object of sacrifices to the gods.

Lamb

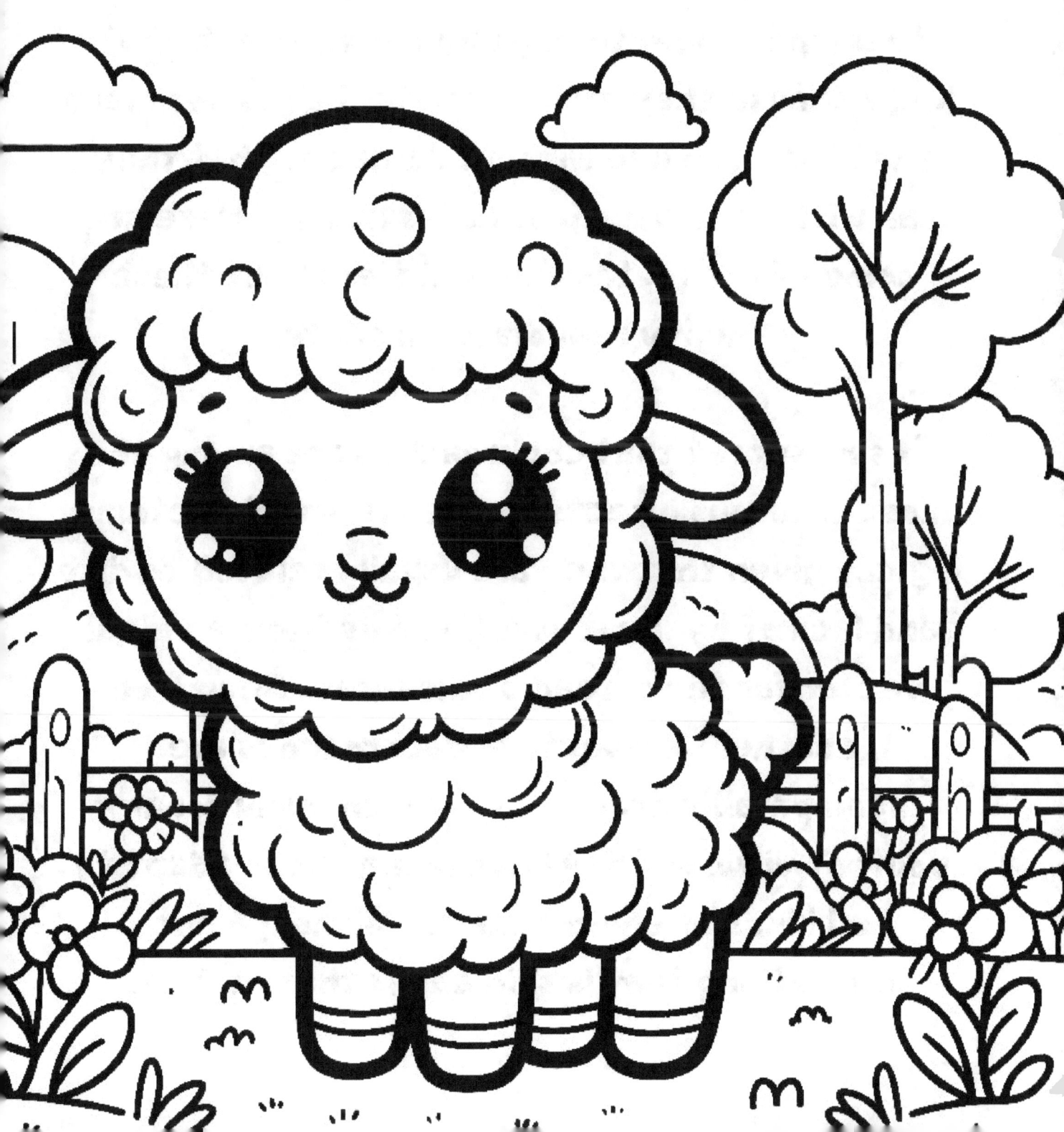

Cockroach

Cockroaches are incomparable creatures from an evolutionary point of view, as they have managed to adapt to practically any environment. But just because they are so resistant does not mean that they can live without a head or that they can withstand a nuclear catastrophe. Here are some of the myths and realities about these highly repudiated insects.

It's no secret that cockroaches are among the most infamous insects on the planet. Something logical, given that they are usually related to dirt and lack of hygiene, which makes them an ideal vector for the spread of diseases. Seen from another perspective, cockroaches are incomparable creatures from an evolutionary point of view, as they have managed to adapt to all kinds of environments. Although not everything that is said about them is true.

Cockroach

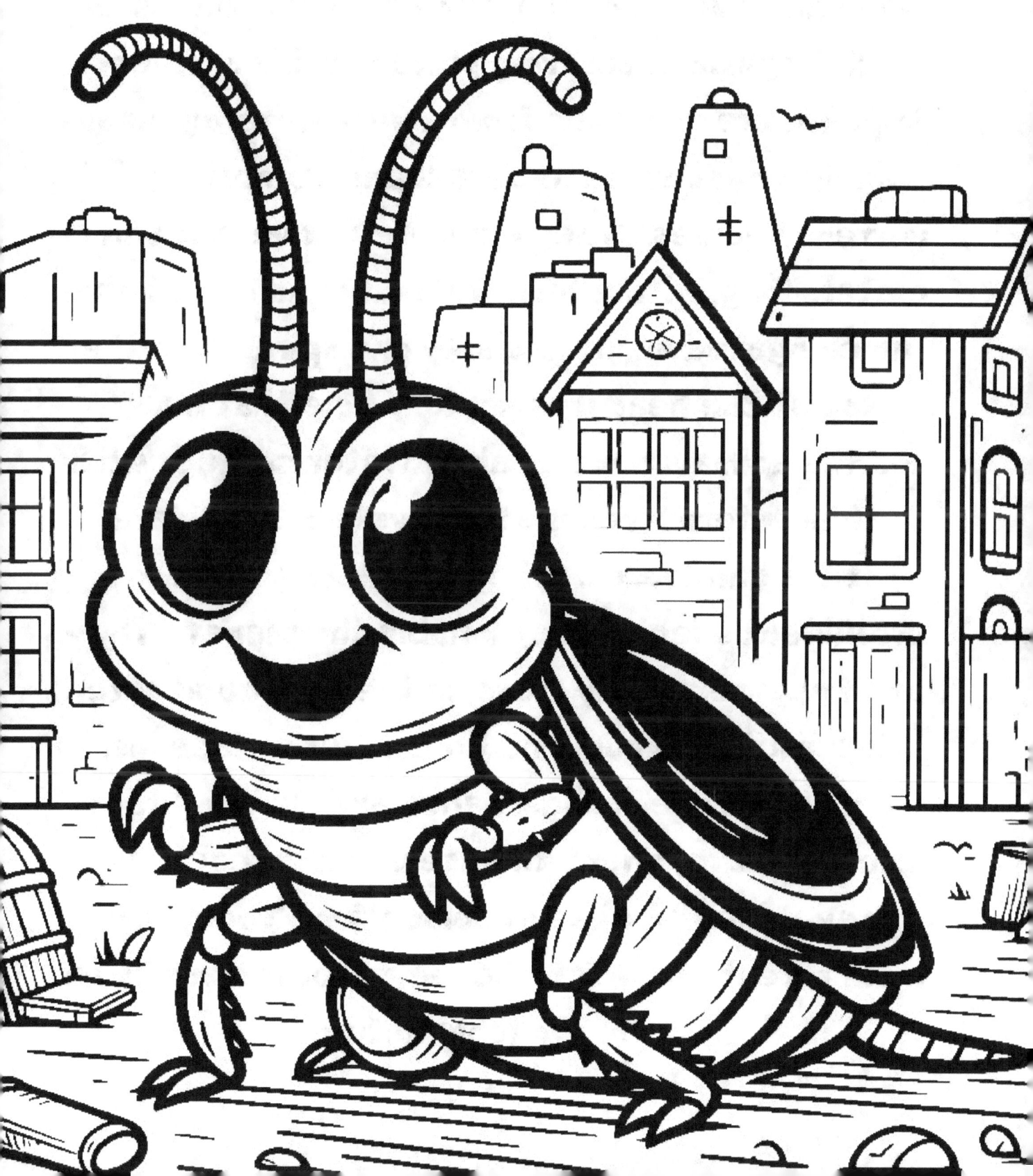

Dolphin

Dolphins (Delphinidae), also oceanic dolphins to distinguish them from platanistoids or river dolphins, are mammals from a very heterogeneous family of odontocete cetaceans, comprising 37 current species. They measure between 2 and 8 meters long, with a fusiform body and large head, an elongated snout and only one spiracle on the top of the head (respiratory hole that many marine animals have as air or water contact with their internal respiratory system). They are strict carnivores. They are among the most intelligent species that inhabit the planet. They are found relatively close to the coast and often interact with humans. Like other cetaceans, dolphins use sounds, dance and jumping to communicate, orient themselves and reach their prey; They also use echolocation. Today, the main threats to which they are exposed are of an anthropogenic nature.

Dolphin

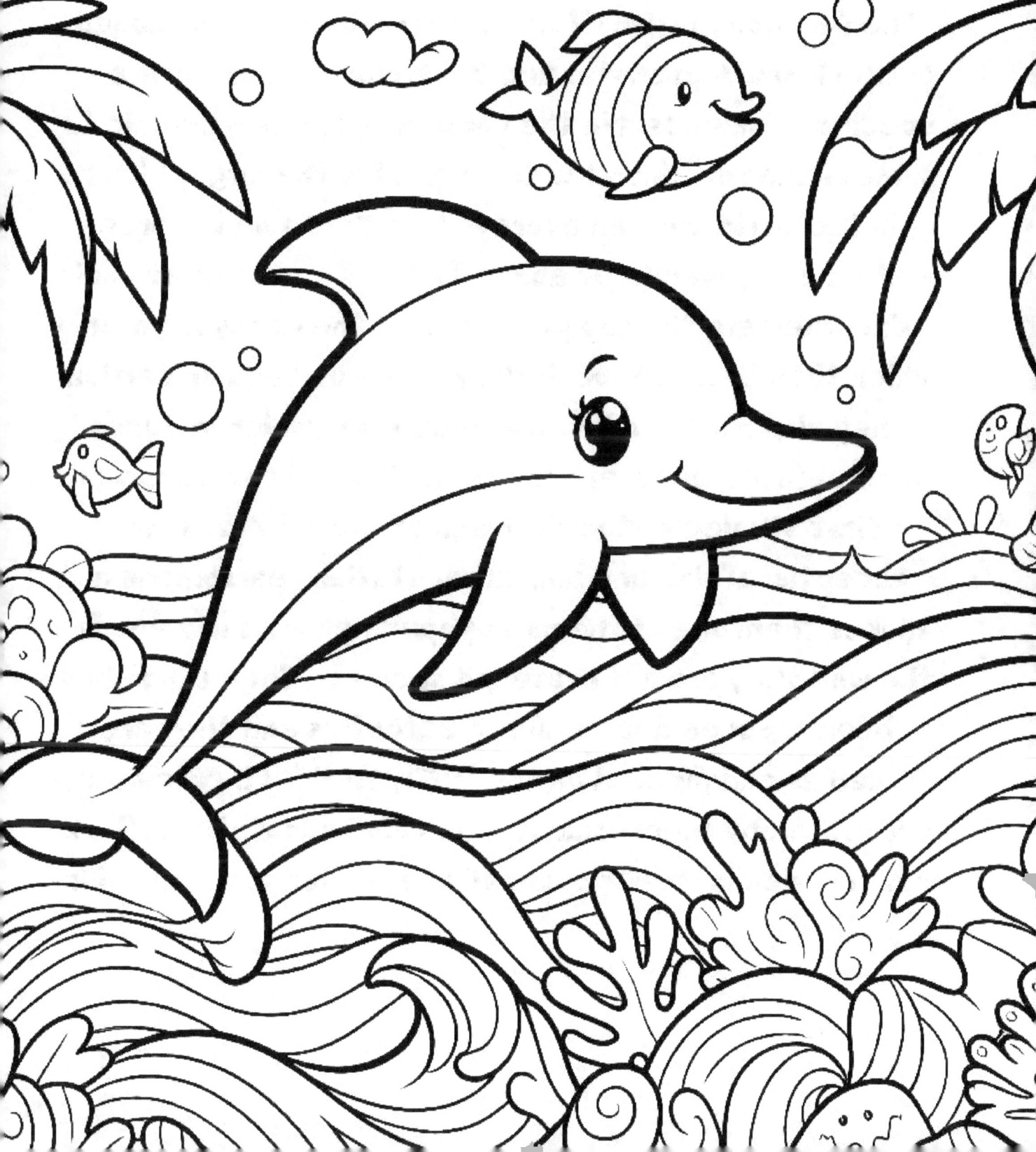

Komodo dragon

The Komodo dragon (Varanus komodoensis), also called the Komodo monster and the Komodo monitor, is a species of sauropsid in the varanidae family, endemic to some islands in central Indonesia. It is the largest lizard in the world, with an average length of two to three meters and a weight of about 70 kg. As a result of their size, they are the top predators of the ecosystems in which they live. Although they primarily feed on carrion, they also hunt and ambush their prey, which includes invertebrates, birds, and mammals. Komodo dragons were first studied by Western scientists in 1910. Their exceptional size and animal reputation fearsomeness makes them one of the most popular animals in zoos. In the wild they are a threatened species; Their range has been reduced due to human activities and they are listed as endangered on the IUCN Red List. They are protected by Indonesian law, and Komodo National Park was founded in 1980 to contribute to their conservation.

Komodo dragon

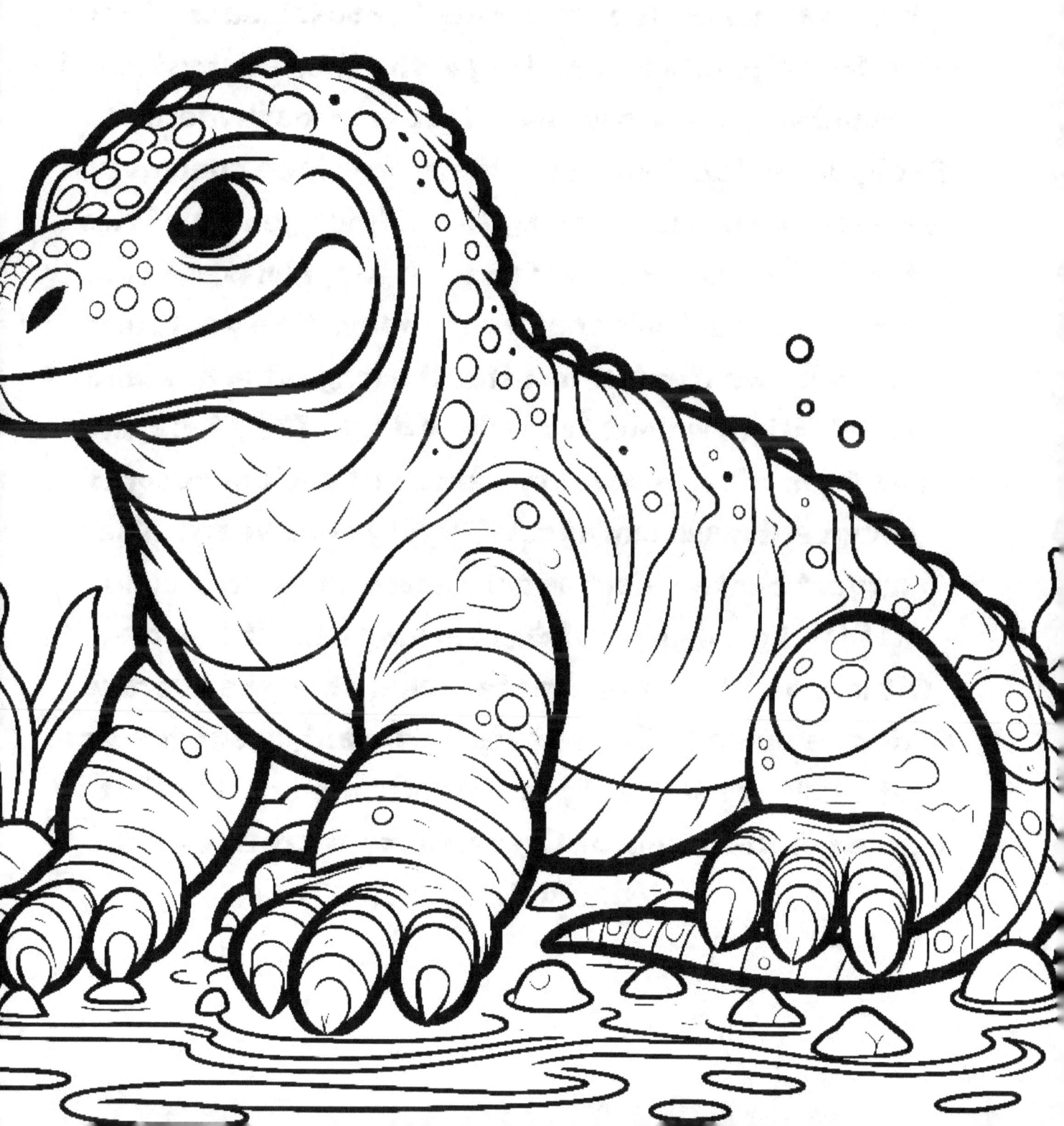

Elephant

Elephants or alopecia (Alopecia) are a family of placental mammals of the order Proboscideans. They were formerly classified, along with other thick-skinned mammals, in the now invalid order of pachyderms (Pachydermata). Nowadays there are three species and several subspecies. Among the extinct genera of this family, the mammoths stand out. Elephants are the largest land animals that exist today. The gestation period is twenty-two months, the longest in any land animal. Birth weight is usually 118 kg. They typically live from fifty to seventy years, but ancient records document maximum ages of eighty-two years. The largest hunted elephant on record weighed around 11,000 kg (Angola, 1956), reaching a height at the withers of 3.96 m, one meter taller than the average African elephant. The smallest elephant, about the size of a calf or a large pig, is a prehistoric species that existed on the island of Crete, Elephas creticus, during the Pleistocene.

Elephant

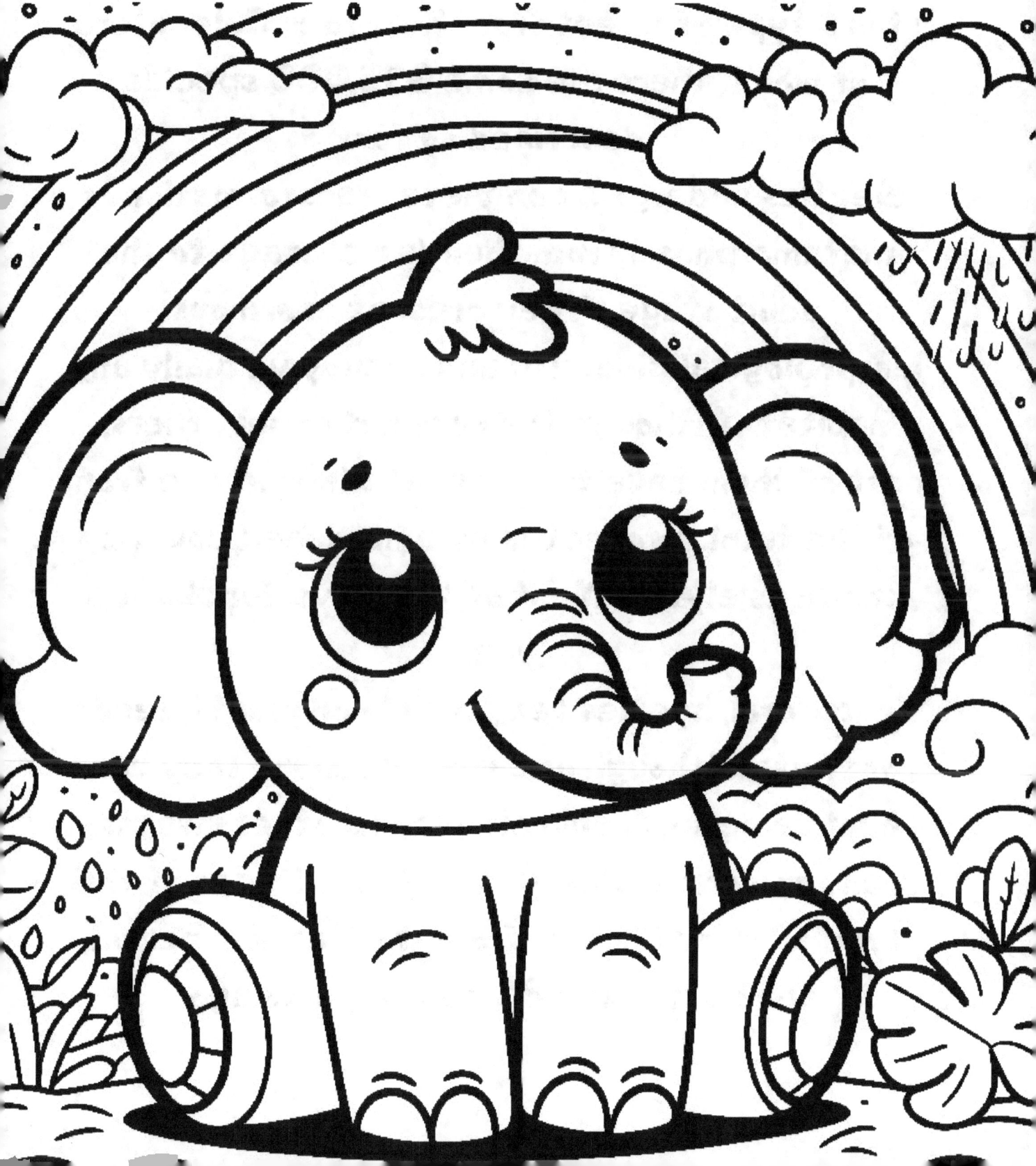

Beetle

It is a type of insect from the order Coleoptera of which there are some 375,000 species described so far.

Beetles undergo a complete transformation or metamorphosis from their larval stage to the adult stage. They present enormous morphological diversity and occupy virtually any habitat. Although they are not expert fliers, most of them have two pairs of wings at the front of the trunk, protected by a hardened covering known as elytra. Most of them live for about a year.

In general, beetles feed mainly on plants, seeds or fruits, although on some occasions they can hunt some small animals such as other insects, snails or worms. One of the oldest traces of this type of animal comes from the Permian period, that is, about 280 million years ago.

Beetle

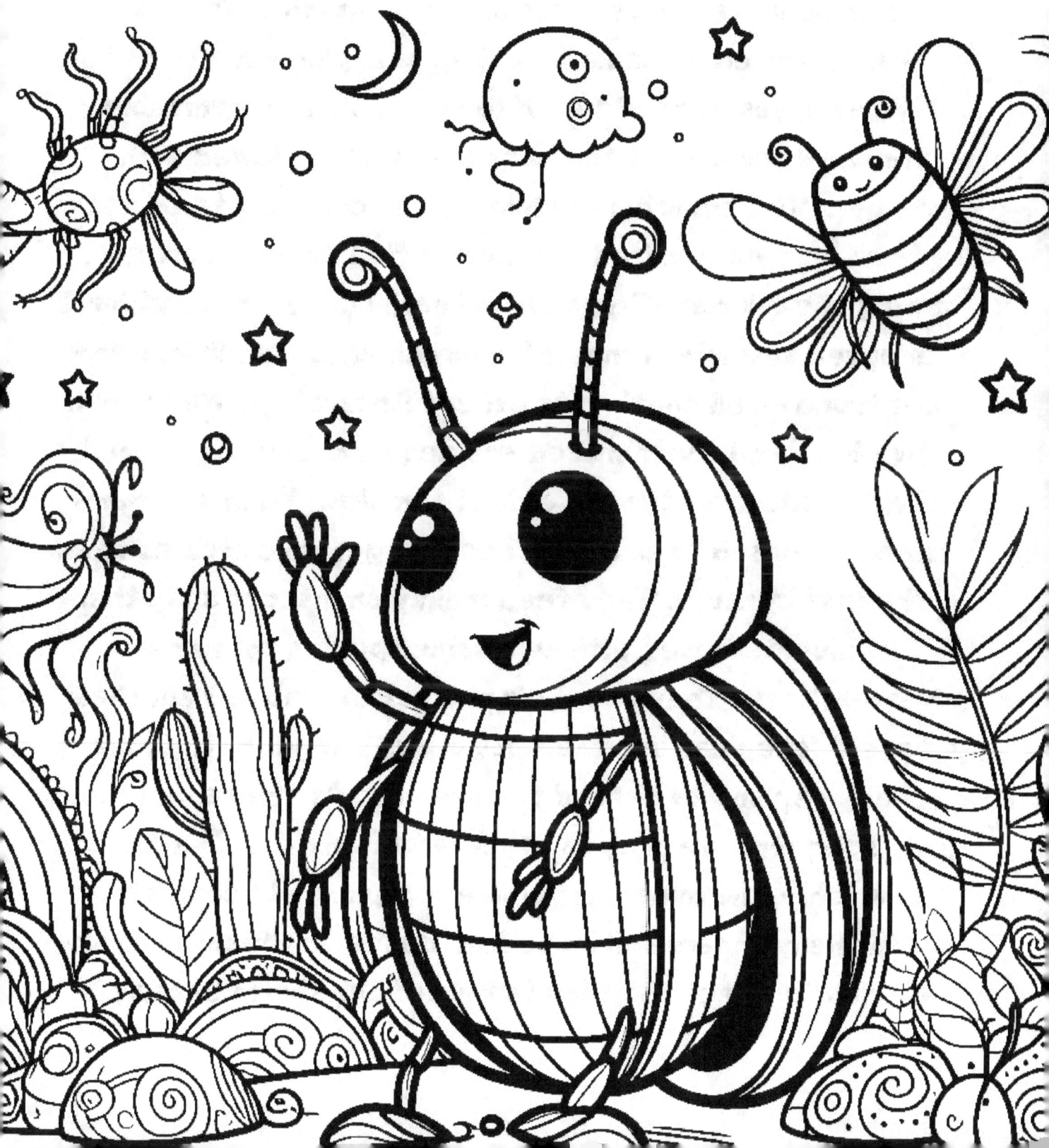

Scorpion

Scorpions are an order of predatory arachnid arthropods commonly known as scorpions or scorpions. They are characterized by having a pair of grasping pincers and a narrow, segmented tail, often forming a recognizable forward curve over the back and always topped with a stinger. The evolutionary history of scorpions dates back to about four hundred and thirty-five million years ago, during the Silurian. They live primarily in deserts, but have adapted to a wide range of environmental conditions and are found on all continents except Antarctica. More than two thousand five hundred species have been described, divided into twenty-two extant families. Their taxonomy is being revised to take into account genomic studies from the 21st century. They feed mainly on insects and other invertebrates, although some species consume vertebrates. They use their pincers to grab and kill their prey. They can use their poisonous stinger both to kill their prey and to defend themselves. At the same time, scorpions are prey to other larger animals. During courtship, the male and female scorpion hold each other with their pincers and move in a "dance" in which the male tries to direct the female toward her sperm capsule.

Scorpion

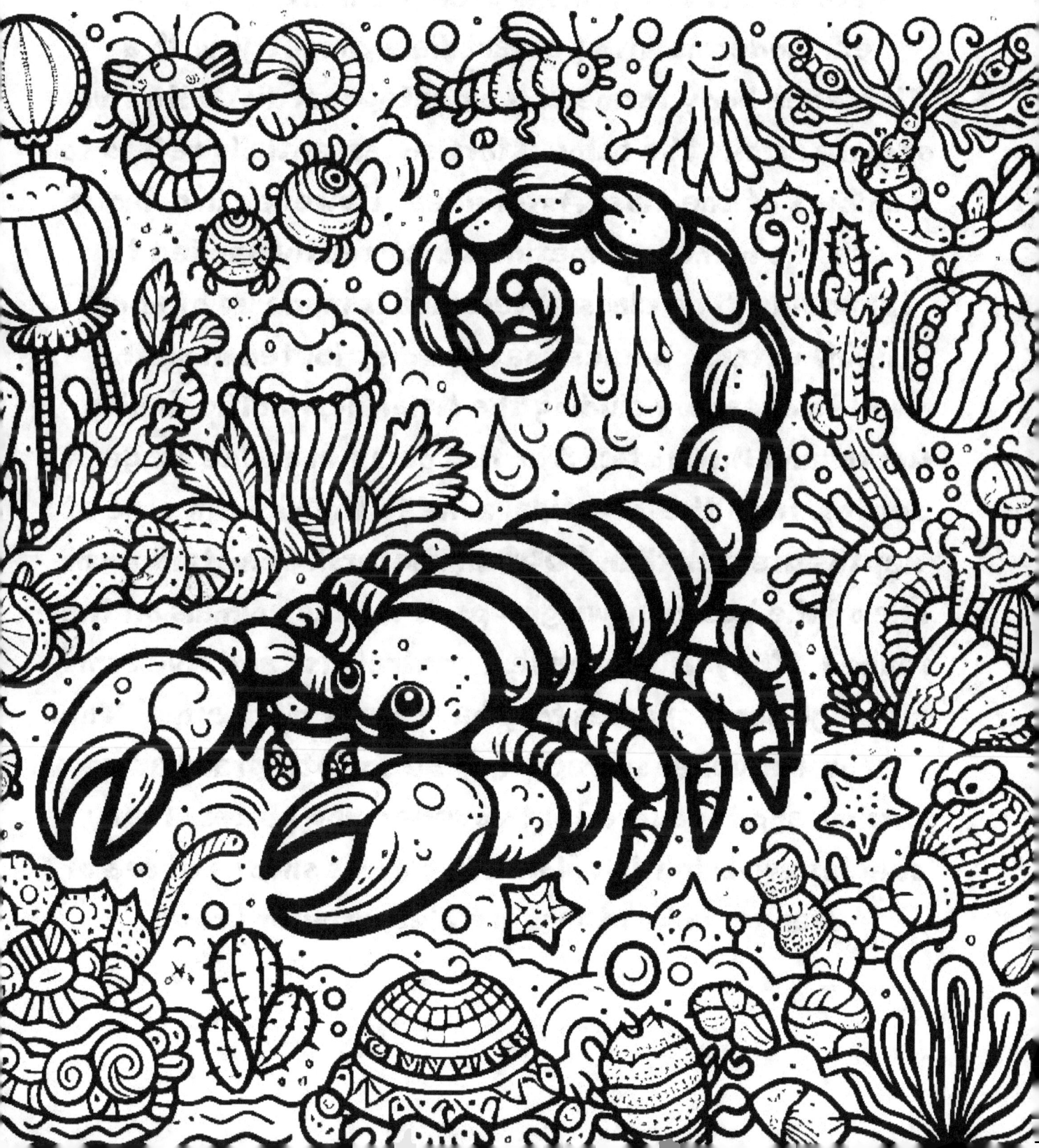

Starfish

Starfish or asteroids (Asteroidea) are a class of echinoderms with pentaradial symmetry, with a flattened body formed by a pentagonal disk with five or more arms. The name "starfish" essentially refers to members of the class Asteroidea. However, in common use the name is sometimes incorrectly applied to ophiuroids. The class Asteroidea is made up of about 1900 extant species that are distributed in all the world's oceans, including the Atlantic, Pacific, Indian, Arctic and Antarctic. Starfish occur in a wide range of depths, from the intertidal zone to the abyssal zone at depths greater than 6000 m (meters). Sea stars form one of the best-known groups of marine animals on the seabed. They usually have a central disc and five arms, although some species may have many more arms. The aboral or upper surface may be smooth, granular or spiny, and is covered with overlapping plates. Many species are brightly colored in various shades of red or orange, while others are blue, gray, or brown.

Starfish

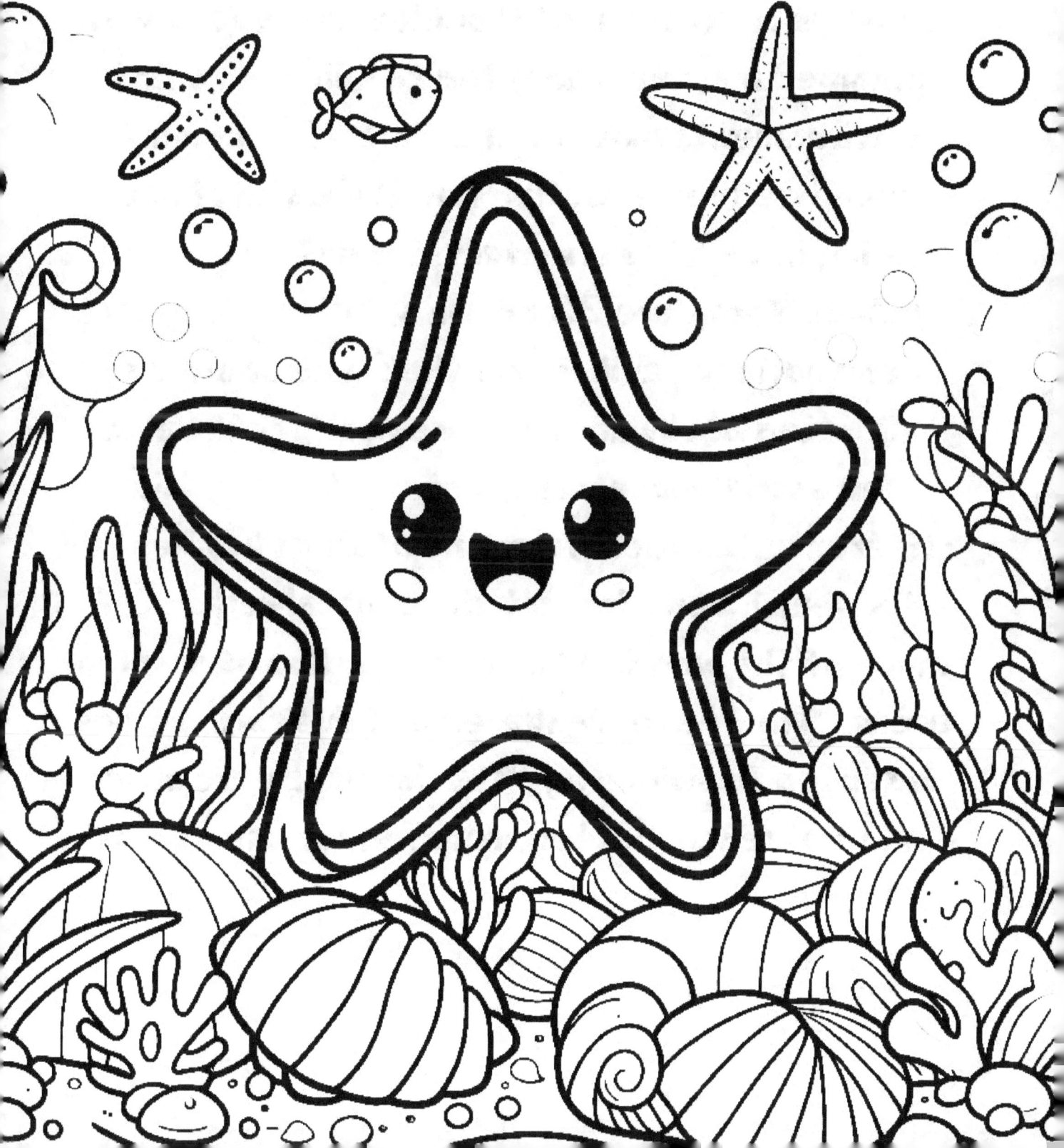

Seal

Phocids or true seals (Phocidae) are a family of pinniped mammals adapted to living in aquatic environments most of the time. The common name derives directly from the Latin phoca, which in turn has its origin in the Greek φώκη (phókē). There are 33 known species. They lack an auditory pavilion and their hind limbs are directed backwards and are not functional in terrestrial movement, a characteristic that differentiates them from the otariids (wolves and fur seals). Seals inhabit the coastal regions of much of the world, with the exception of tropical areas. They have elongated and fusiform bodies, adapted to swimming; The forelimbs are short and flattened, better prepared for use as fins.

Seal

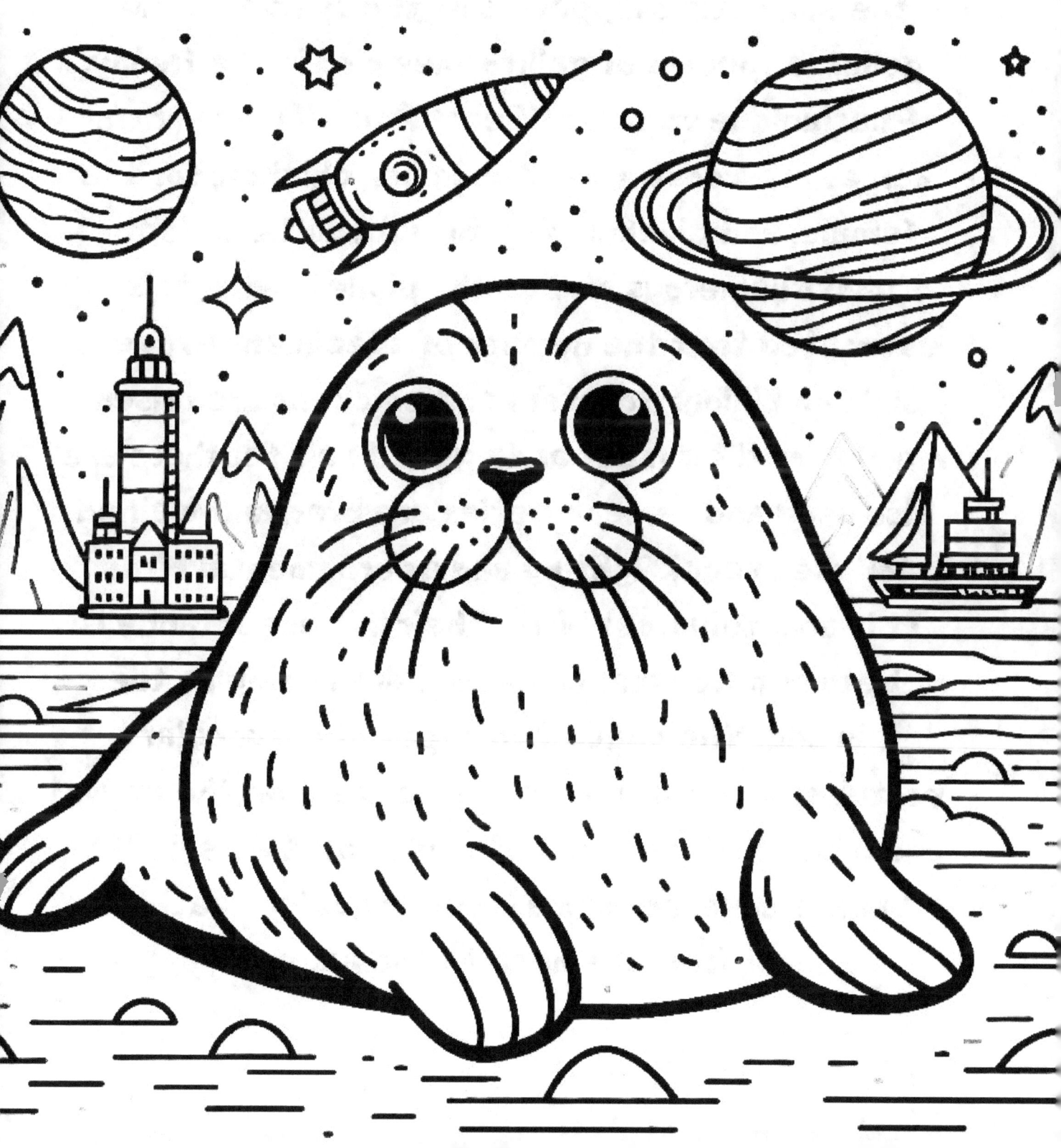

Hen

The rooster and hen (Gallus gallus domesticus) are the domestic subspecies of the species Gallus gallus, a species of galliformes bird in the family Phasianidae from Southeast Asia. The common names are: rooster, for the male; chicken, for the female, and chicken, for the subadults. It is the most numerous bird on the planet, since it is estimated that the number of specimens exceeds sixteen billion. Roosters and chickens are raised mainly for their meat and eggs. Their feathers are also used and some varieties are bred and trained for use in cockfighting and as ornamental birds. It is an omnivorous bird. Their life expectancy is between five and ten years, depending on the breed. They have two types of caruncular protuberances on their heads: a crest on the crown and lobes that hang on both sides of the beak. The back is covered with a layer of golden feathers from the neck to the back.

Hen

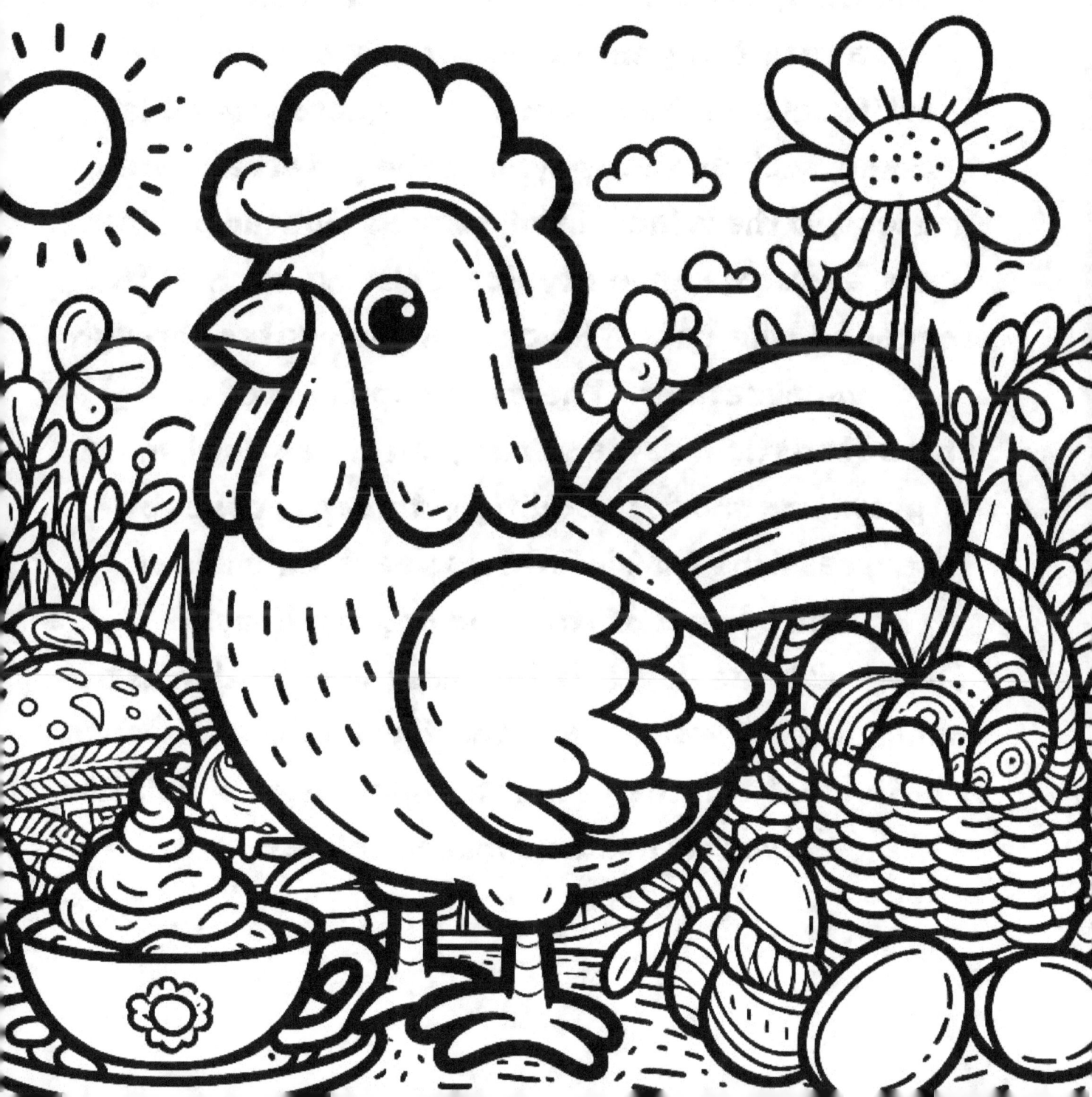

Cat

The current name in many languages comes from the Vulgar Latin catus. Paradoxically, catus alluded to wild cats, while domestic cats were called felis. As a result of genetic mutations, crossing and artificial selection, there are numerous breeds. Some, such as the sphynx or the peterbald, are hairless; Others lack a tail, such as Bobtail or Manx cats, and some have atypical coloring, such as the so-called blue cats. The cat communicates through vocalizations. The most popular are its characteristic meow and purr, but it can howl, moan, growl and snort. In addition, it adopts poses or expressions that inform its peers, enemies or caregivers of its mood or intentions.
Along with the dog, it is the most popular domestic animal as a pet, as an aid in the fight against rodents, or both. In 2017, the estimated global cat population was six hundred million felines.

Cat

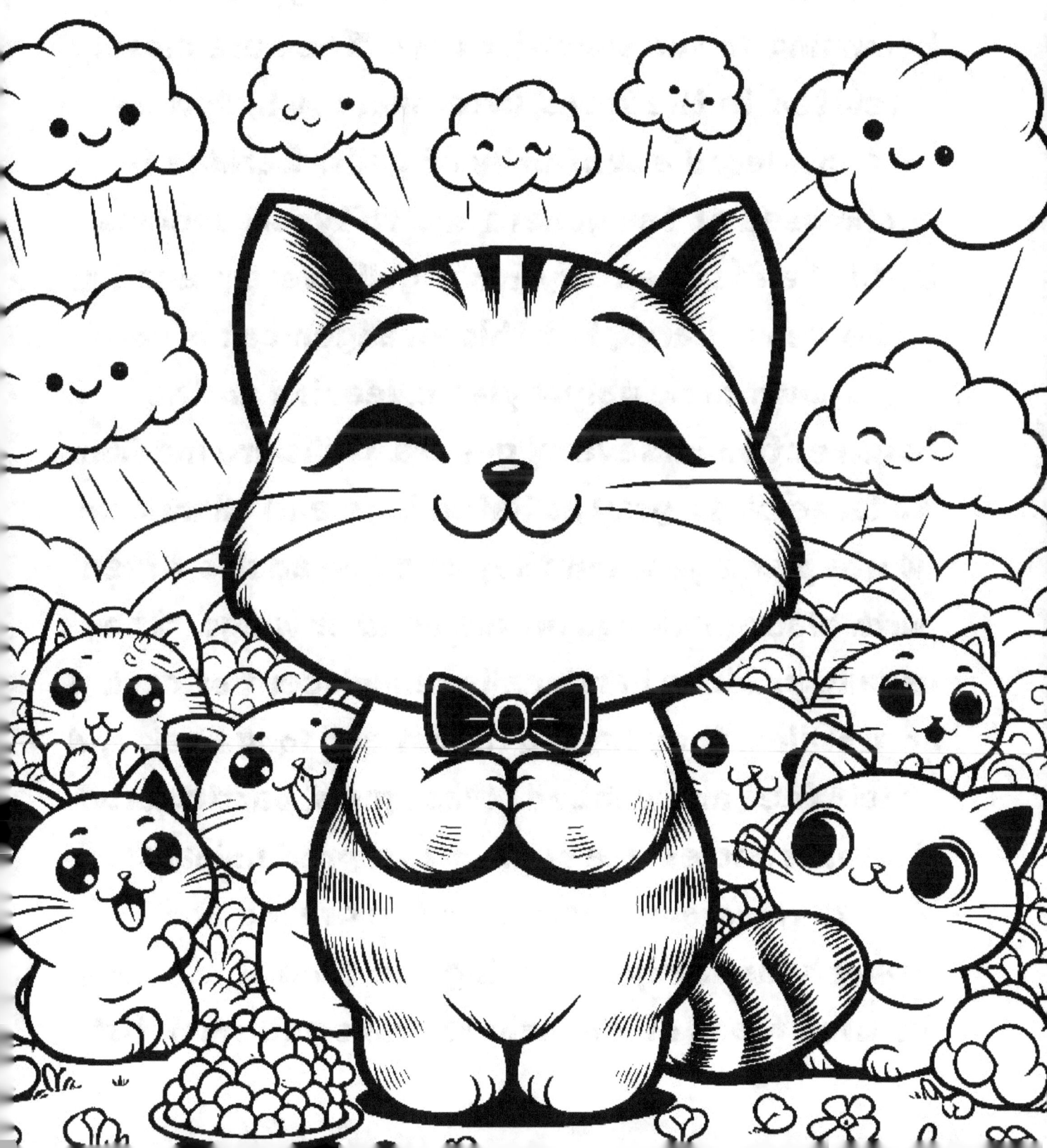

Seagull

Seagulls are a group of birds classified within the order Charadriiformes and family Laridae, belonging to the suborder Lari. They are closely related to the terns, (Sternidae), which were considered a subfamily of gulls. Laridae is composed of ten genera and fifty-six species. Until the 21st century, most gulls were placed in the genus Larus, but this arrangement is now known to be polyphyletic, leading to the resurrection of several genera. Gulls are medium to large birds, gray as hatchlings. and change to white plumage when they become adults, often with black markings on the head or wings. They usually produce harsh calls reminiscent of crying or growling, they have a robust and long beak and their feet are webbed. Most gulls, particularly Larus species, are omnivorous, predominantly carnivorous, nesting on the ground and opportunistically capturing live food or stealing it. Live foods often include crabs and small fish.

Seagull

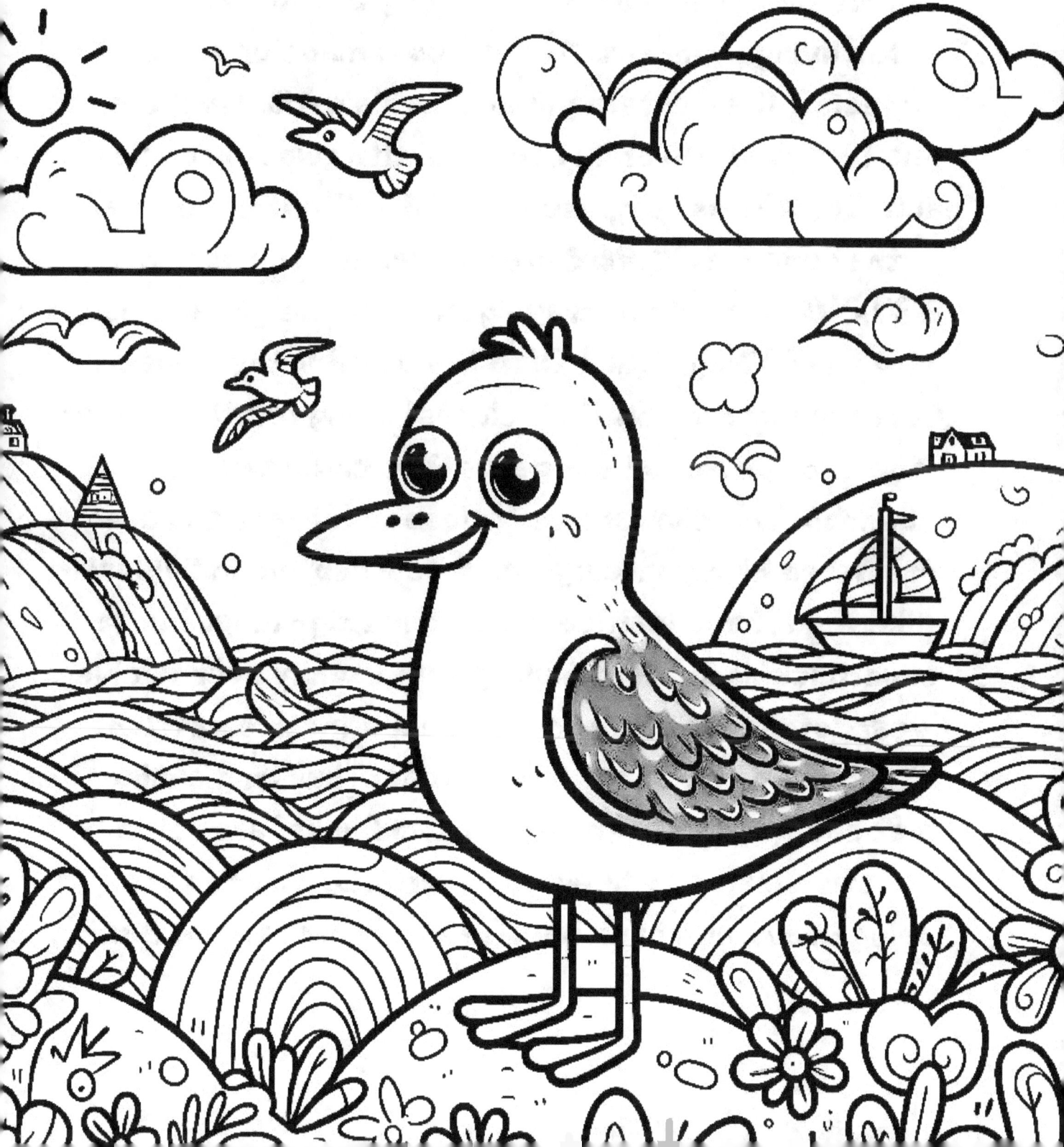

Gorilla

Gorillas (genus Gorilla) are herbivorous primates that inhabit the forests of Africa. They are the largest of the living primates. The genus is made up of two species: the western gorilla (Gorilla gorilla) and the eastern gorilla (Gorilla beringei) with two subspecies each. Its DNA is composed of 3,041,976,159 base pairs that encode 20,962 protein genes composed of 237,216 exons. An average gorilla can weigh between 140 and 180 kg. Their DNA is 97-98% the same as that of humans, being their closest living relatives after the two species of the genus Pan (chimpanzees and bonobos). Gorillas are very close to humans and are considered highly intelligent. A few captive individuals, like Koko, have learned a simplified sign language. A "silverback" is an adult male gorilla, usually over twelve years of age, and named for the distinctive patch of silver hair on its back. A "silverback" has long canines that emerge with maturity. "Blackbacks" are sexually active males up to eleven years old. Gorillas are polygamous, and have been seen mating face to face.

Gorilla

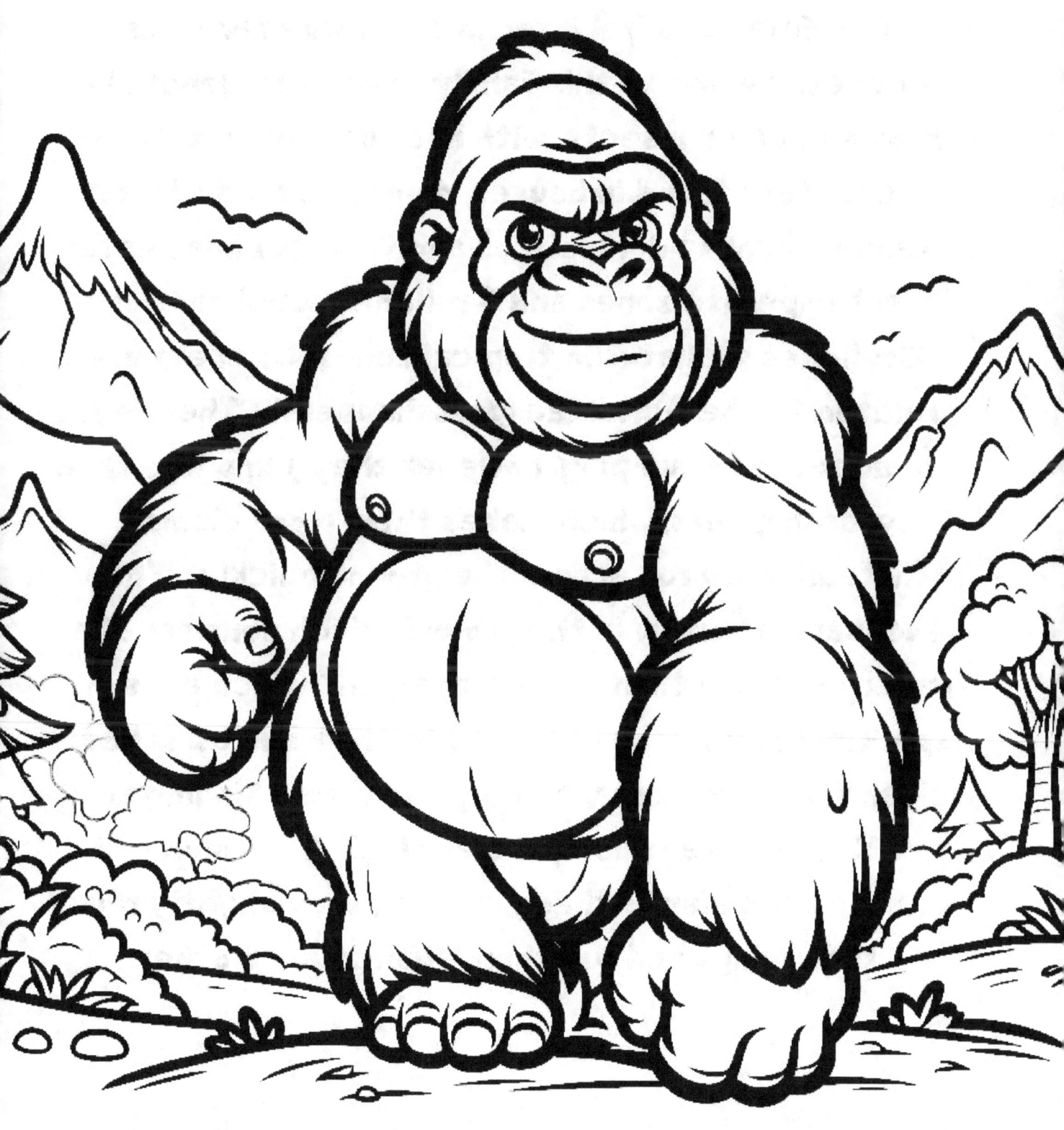

Cricket

Grillids (Gryllidae) are a family of orthopteran insects of the superfamily Grylloidea, within the suborder Ensifera. Several insects commonly known as crickets belong to this family. They are generally brown to black insects, with nocturnal habits. Some species are found in houses, domestic crickets, for example *Acheta domesticus* and *Gryllus bimaculatus* in temperate zones and *Gryllodes supplicans* or *Gryllodes sigillatus* in tropical zones. Crickets are related to the Acrididae (grasshoppers). Their legs are adapted to jumping, however they jump less than grasshoppers, which makes them more clumsy. Instead, they run across the ground quickly. They excavate a burrow in the ground, which consists of a gallery of more than half a meter, and which ends in a spherical room. The entrance to their burrow is kept clean for a large area, as they use it as a singing area to attract females (only males sing). To produce the sound so peculiar to these insects, they slightly raise their wings and rub them against each other.

Cricket

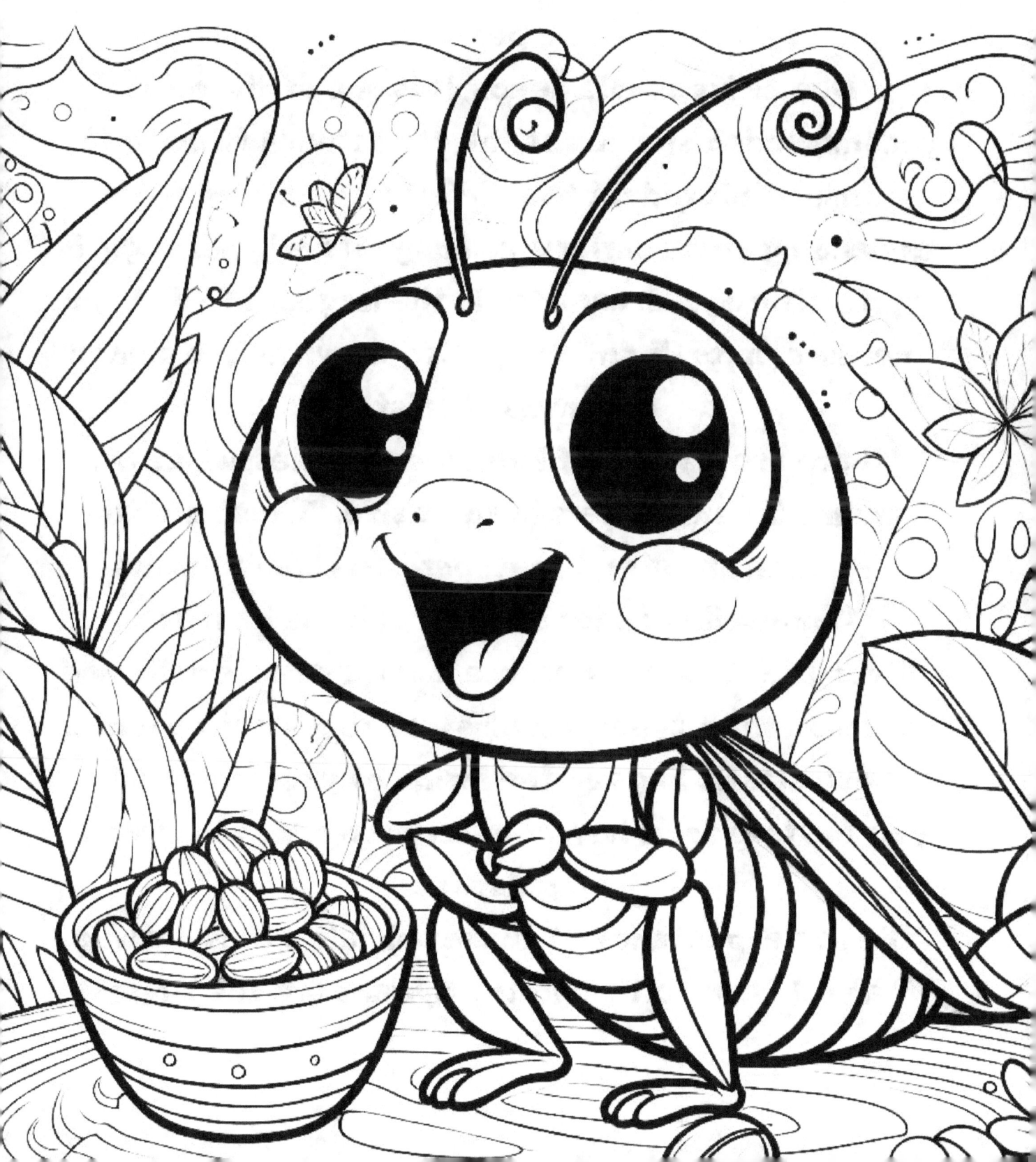

Hamster

The hamster is a small rodent that is widely used as a pet.

Due to its simple needs, it is one of the most recommended species as the first animal to unite the family. This rodent has different points of origin, depending on its variety, although its original origin is Syria. The Syrian hamster is the largest of all, it can measure up to 15 cm, and is also known as the golden or common hamster.

There are also dwarf hamster varieties, which are around 5 centimeters in adult size. These are the Russian hamster, the Roborowski hamster, the Campbell hamster and the Chinese hamster.

Among their curiosities, the most characteristic and common to all types of hamster are pocket pouches. These elastic bags on the inside of your mouth allow you to store food, hay, or other materials you want to transport.

The life expectancy of these animals varies between 2 and 3 years, although the Syrians are the longest.

Hamster

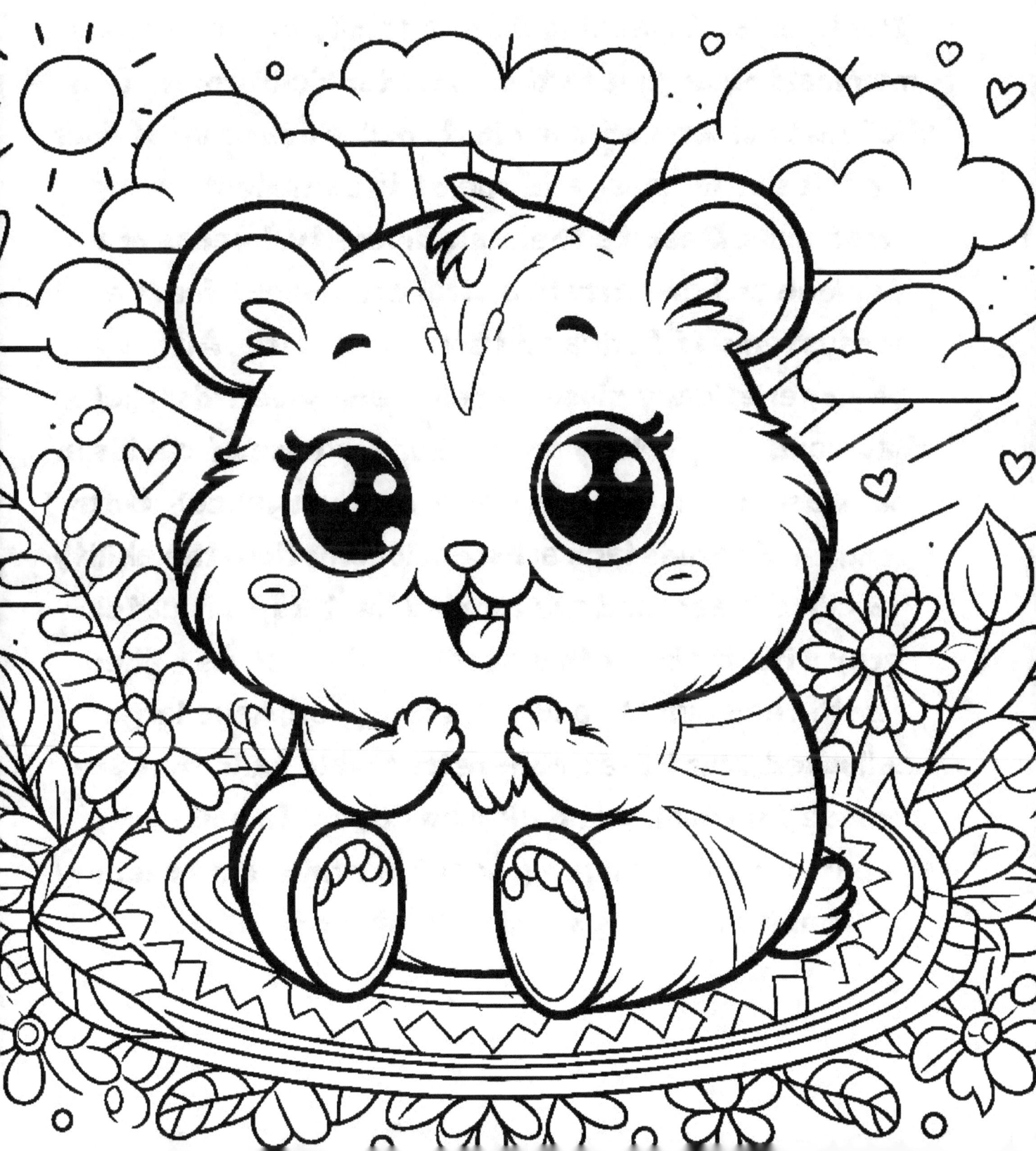

Hyena

The hyenids (Hyaenidae) are a family of carnivorous mammals belonging to the suborder Feliformes. It is the least numerous family in its order (made up of four species of hyenas), and one of the smallest among mammals. Despite their low diversity, hyenas are unique and constitute a vital component for the ecosystems of Africa and some from Asia. Although phylogenetically close to felids and viverrids, their shape and morphology are similar to those of canids in many aspects (see evolutionary convergence); Both hyenas and canids lack arboreal locomotion (the ability to climb trees) and are running hunters that catch prey with their teeth instead of their claws. They both feed quickly and can store food, have large calloused, blunt feet, non-retractable nails that are made for running and digging caves. In any case, hyenas' grooming, marking scent, mating, and breeding habits are consistent with other feliforms.

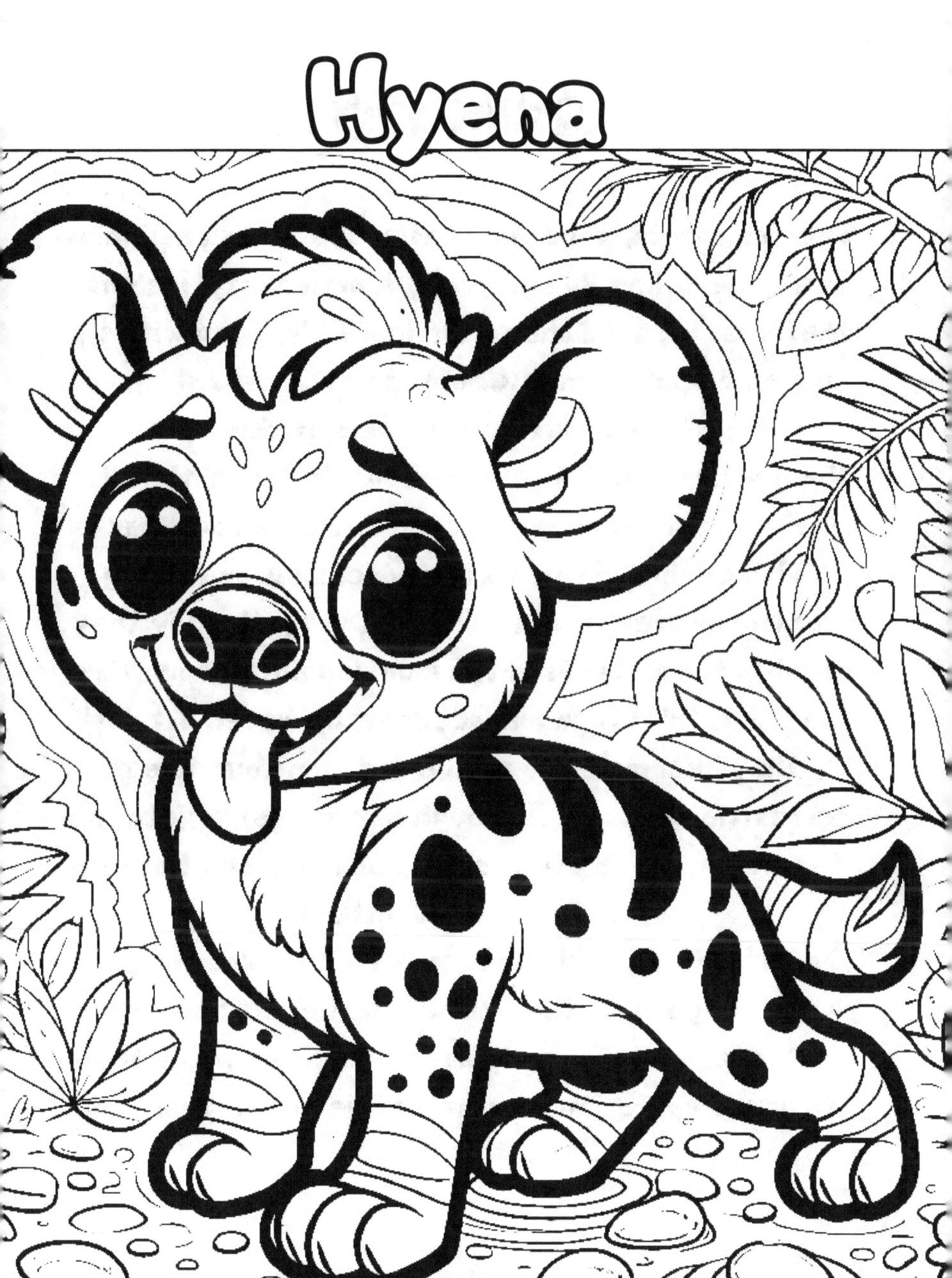

Hippo

The common hippopotamus (Hippopotamus amphibius) is a large, primarily herbivorous, artiodactyl mammal that lives in sub-Saharan Africa. It is, along with the pygmy hippopotamus (Choeropsis liberiensis), one of the only two current members of the family Hippopotamidae. It is a semi-aquatic animal that lives in rivers and lakes and where territorial adult males with groups of five to thirty females and young control an area from the river. During the day they rest in the water or in the mud and both copulation and birth of this animal occur in the water. At dusk they become more active and come out to eat terrestrial grasses. Although hippos rest together in the water, grazing is a solitary activity and they are not territorial on land.

Despite their physical resemblance to pigs and other land ungulates, their closest living relatives are cetaceans (whales, porpoises, etc.) from which they diverged approximately fifty-five million years ago.

Hippo

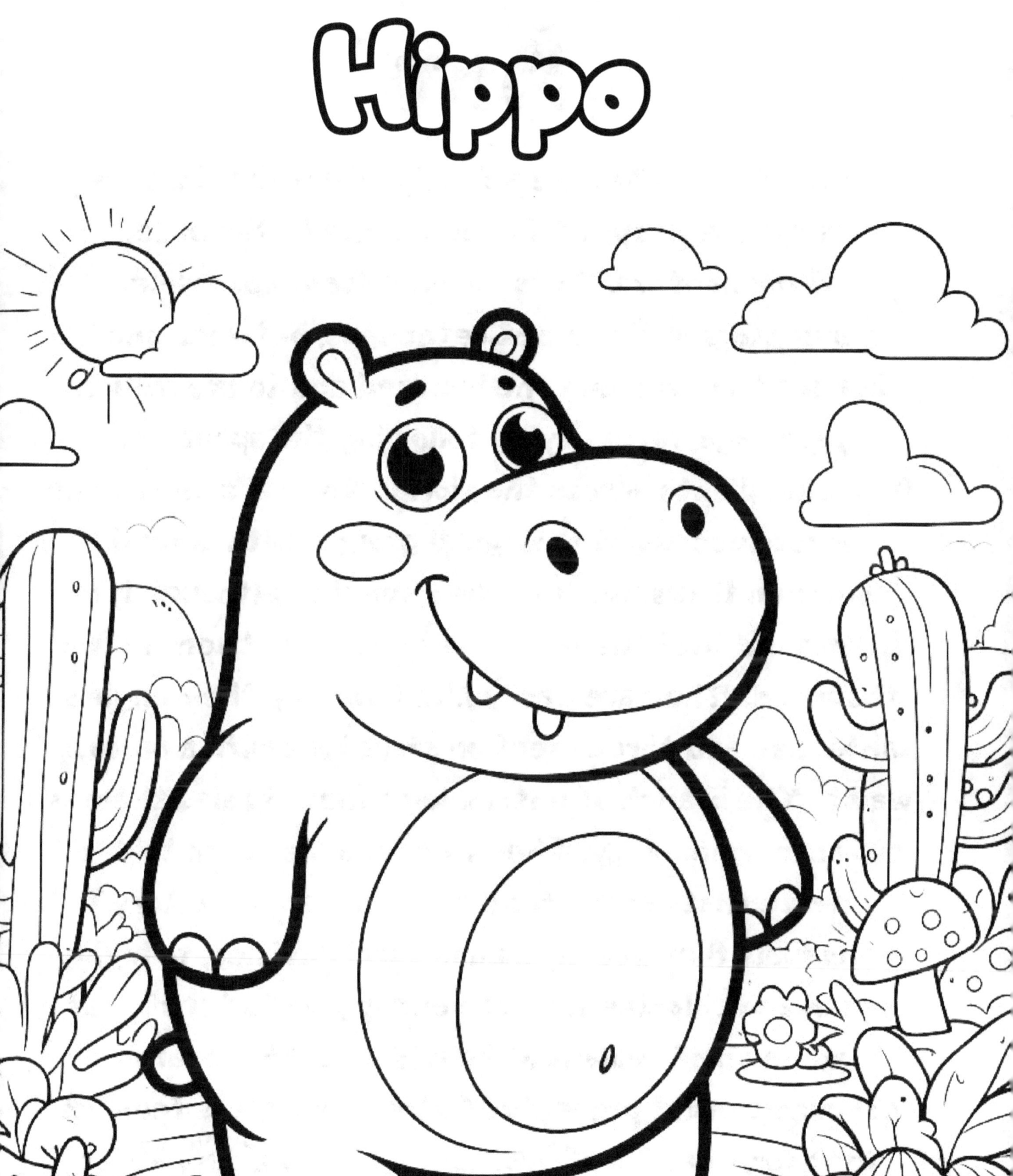

Ant

Ants (Formicidae) are a family of eusocial insects that, like wasps and bees, belong to the order Hymenoptera. Ants evolved from wasp-like ancestors in the mid-Cretaceous, between one hundred and ten and one hundred and thirty million years ago, diversifying following the spread of flowering plants across the world. They are one of the most successful zoological groups, with around fourteen thousand described species, although it is estimated that there may be more than twenty-two thousand. They are easily identified by their angled antennae and three-section structure with a narrow waist. The branch of entomology that studies them is called myrmecology. They form colonies or anthills of a size that ranges from a few dozen predatory individuals that live in small natural cavities, to highly organized colonies that can occupy large territories made up of millions of individuals. These large colonies consist primarily of sterile, wingless females that form castes of "workers," "soldiers," and other specialized groups.

Ant

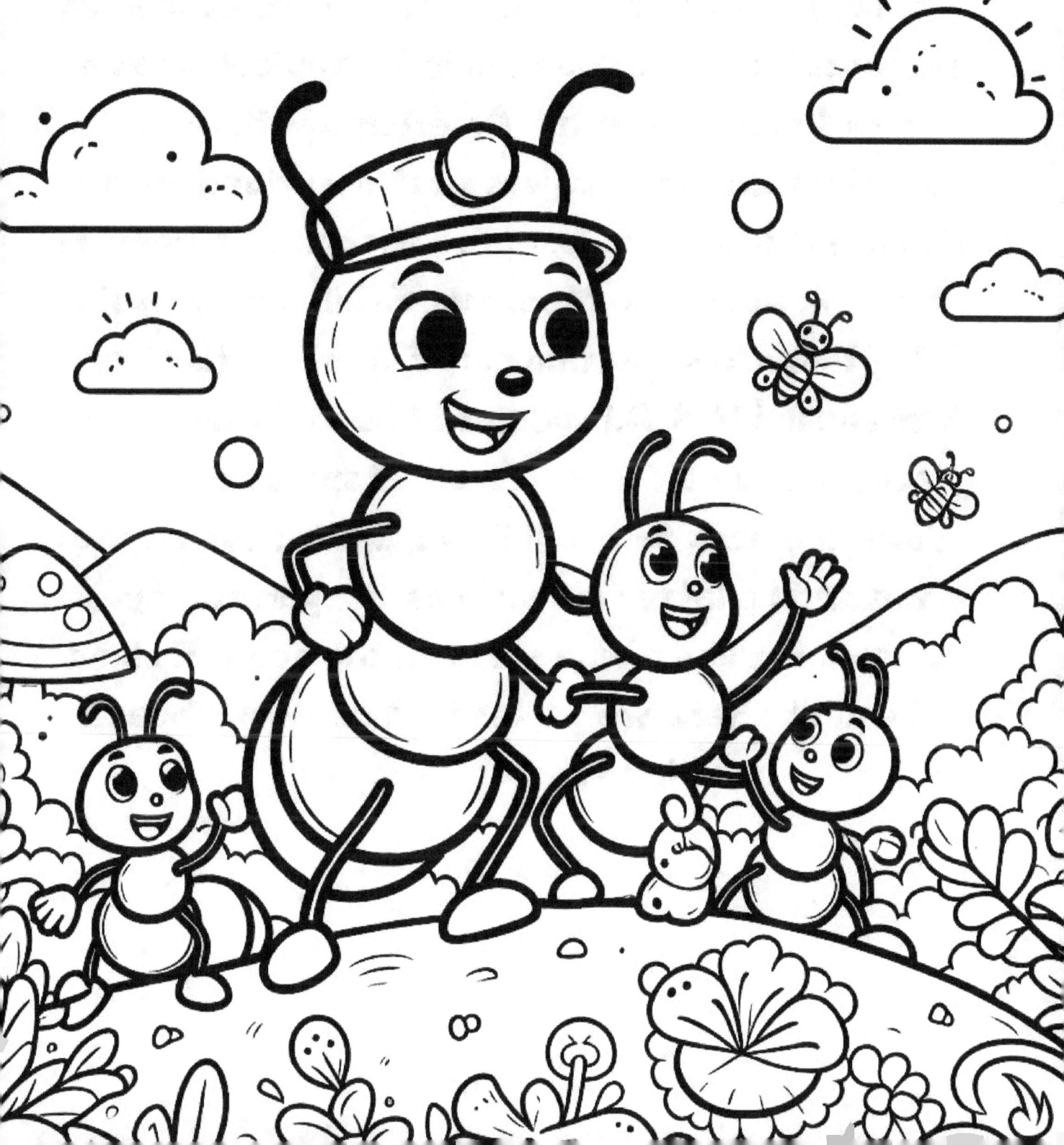

Iguana

True iguanas (Iguana) are a genus of scaly iguanid sauropsids (reptiles), endemic to tropical areas of North America, Central America, South America and the Caribbean. It was first described by the Austrian naturalist Josephus Nicolaus Laurenti in his book Specimen Medicum, Exhibens Synopsin Reptilium Emendatam cum Experimentis circa Venena in 1768. All species of lizard in the genus Iguana have a dewlap, a pair of spines that run down the back to the tail, and a third eye on the head. The latter is known as the parietal eye, which looks like a pale scale on the head. Behind the neck there are scales that resemble beaks, called tubercular scales.

Iguana

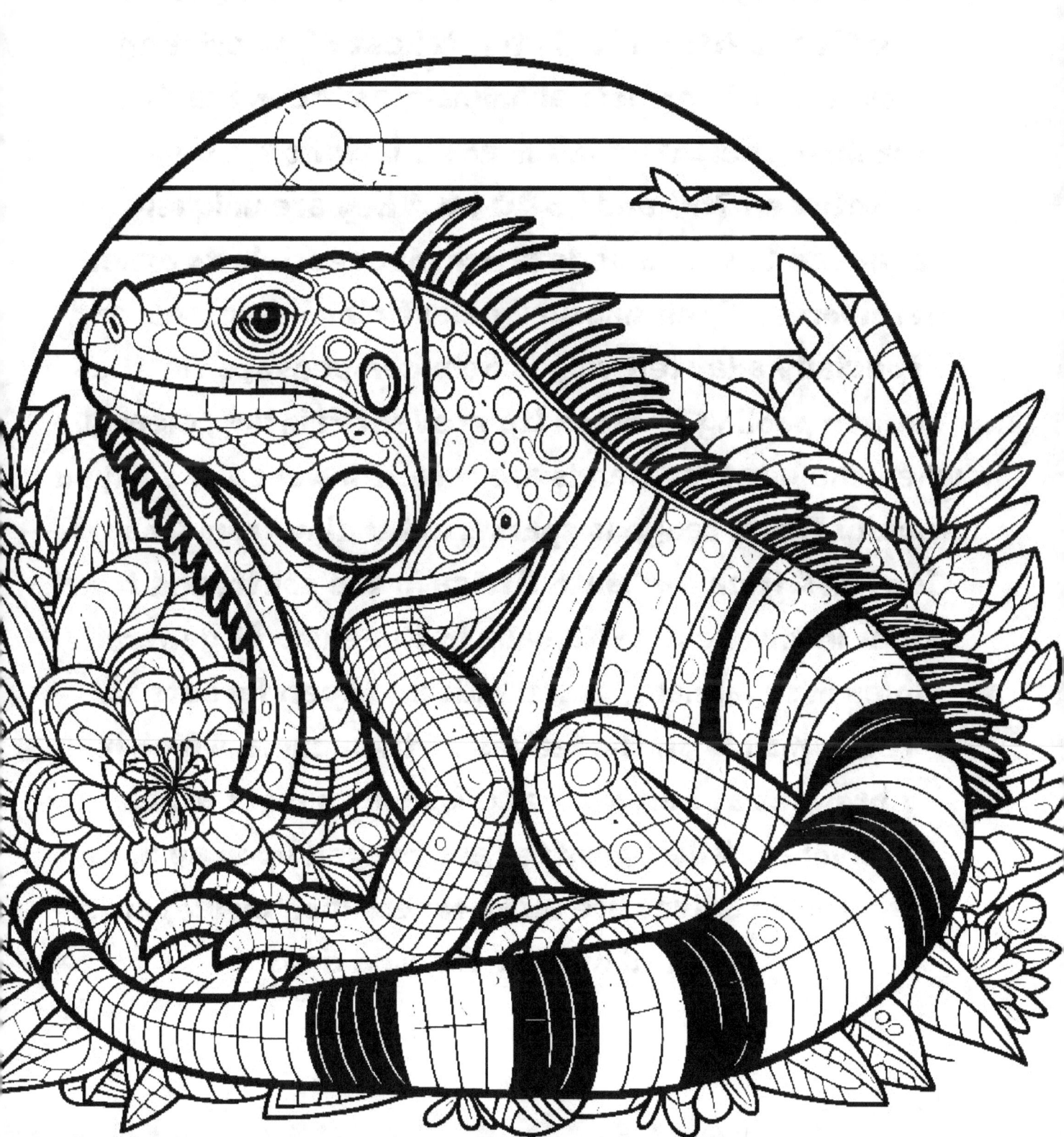

Giraffe

The giraffe (Giraffa camelopardalis) is a species of artiodactyl mammal, from the family Giraffidae, native to Africa. It is the tallest of all existing species of terrestrial animals, as it can reach a maximum height of 5.7 m and a weight that varies between 750 and 1,600 kg. They are uniquely adapted to reach vegetation inaccessible to other herbivores. Their unusually elastic blood vessels and specially adapted valves help compensate for the sudden pooling of blood (to prevent fainting, clearly) when the giraffes' heads are raised, lowered or swayed rapidly. Their range is sparse, extending from Chad in Central Africa, to South Africa in the south, and from Niger in the west to Somalia in the east. It generally lives in savannahs, grasslands and open forests. It feeds mainly on the leaves of the acacia, which it browses at heights inaccessible to most other herbivores. Adult giraffes are preyed upon by lions, and giraffe calves are also preyed upon by leopards, spotted hyenas and wild dogs.

Giraffe

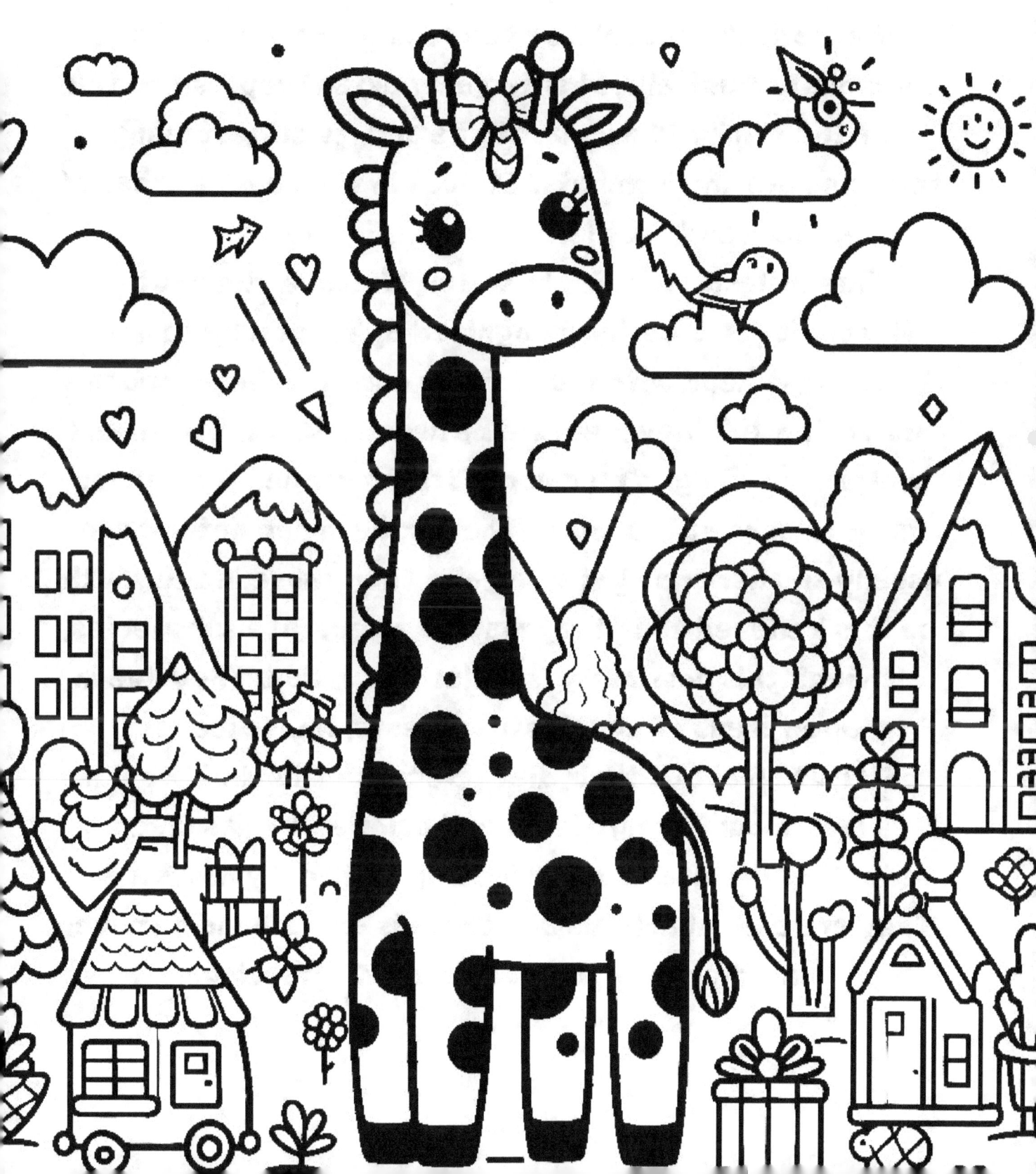

Koala

The koala (Phascolarctos cinereus) is a species of diprotodont marsupial of the family Phascolarctidae, endemic to Australia. It is the only extant representative of the family Phascolarctidae and its closest living relatives are the wombats. It lives in the coastal areas of eastern and southern Australia, in the states of Queensland, New South Wales, Victoria and South Australia. It is easily recognized by its stocky tailless body, large head with round, furry ears, and large, spoon-shaped nose. They measure between 60 and 85 cm and weigh 4 to 15 kg. The color of its fur ranges from silver gray to chocolate brown. The northern populations are usually smaller and lighter in color than those in the south, so it is believed that they may be a separate subspecies, although this possibility is under discussion. They live in open areas of eucalyptus forests, whose leaves constitute most of their diet. Because this diet provides a low amount of nutrients and calories, koalas lead a sedentary life and usually sleep up to twenty hours a day. They are asocial animals and there is only a bond between mothers and their dependent offspring.

Koala

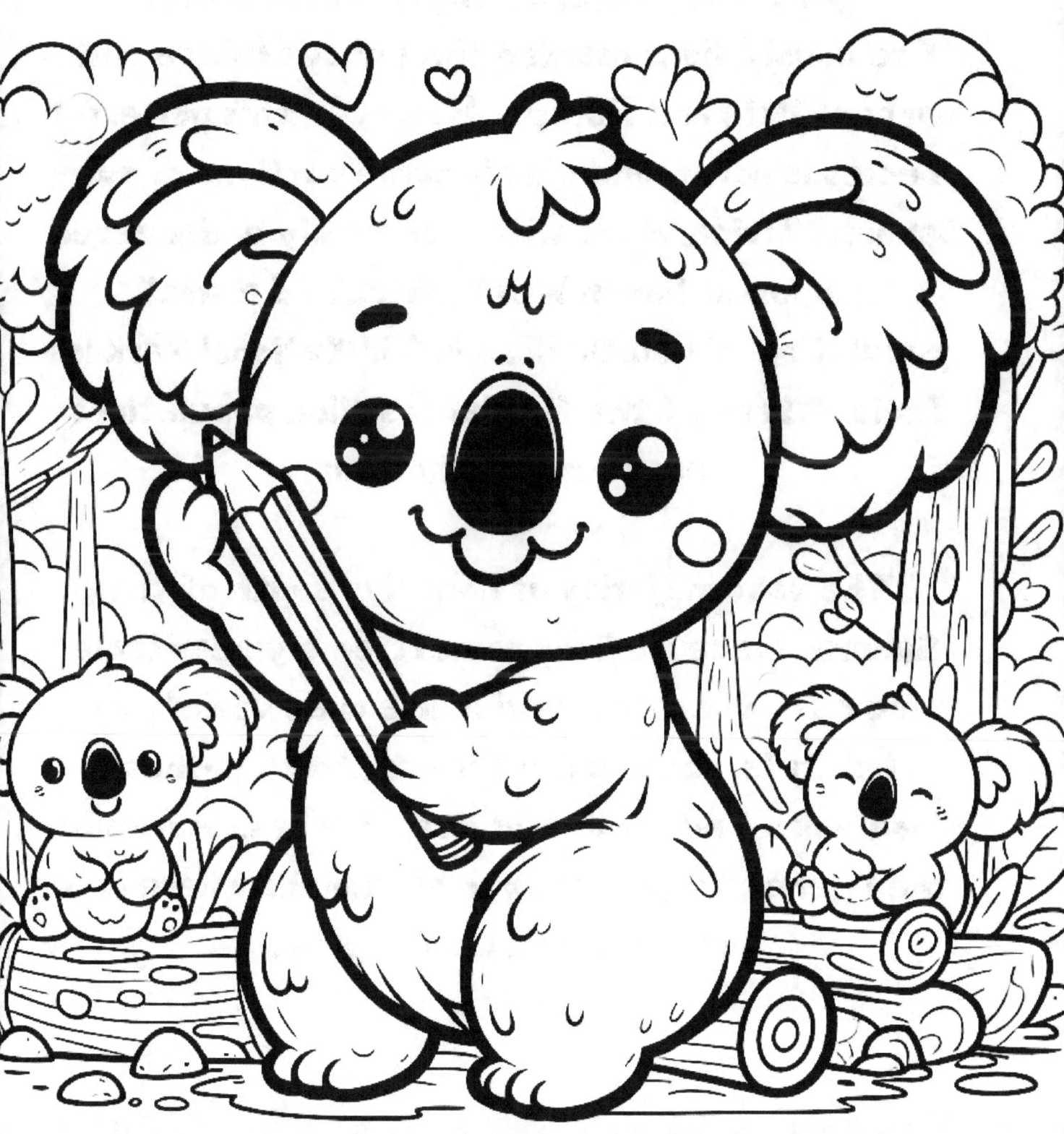

Lion

Throughout history, lions have been admired as a symbol of power, strength and bravery. Previously, lions roamed throughout Africa and parts of Asia and Europe. However, this powerful species is now found only in some portions of sub-Saharan Africa, along with a critically endangered subpopulation in West Africa and a small population of Asiatic lions in Gir National Park in India. Three of the five largest lion populations are found in Tanzania.

The vast majority of lions live south of the Sahara. Because lions are extremely adaptable big cats, they can survive in a wide variety of habitats, such as dry forests, thick bushes, floodplains, and semi-arid desert areas. However, they generally prefer open savannahs where it is easier to stalk their prey.

Lion

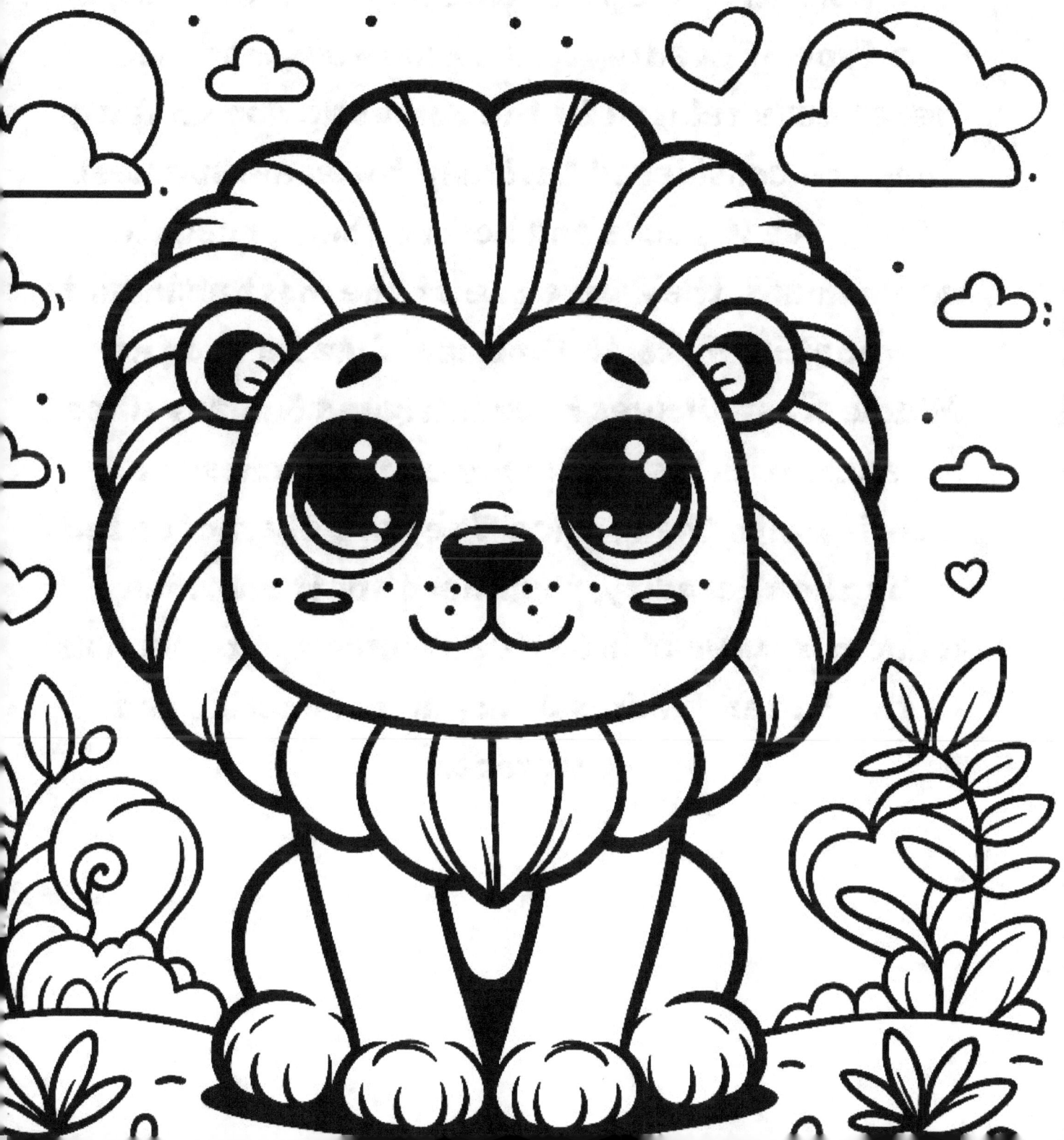

Wolf

The wolf, with the scientific name Canis lupus, is a type of quadrupedal carnivorous mammal, genetically related to the domestic dog (in fact, they are considered basically the same species). They live in packs and before their encounter with humans, they were one of the most abundant predators in North America, Eurasia and the Middle East. Wolves have intrigued humans since ancient times, and many cultures chose to identify with them, since They are characterized by their ferocity, their herd spirit and their tenacious survival in hostile environments, such as the frozen tundras of northern America and Europe.

Wolf

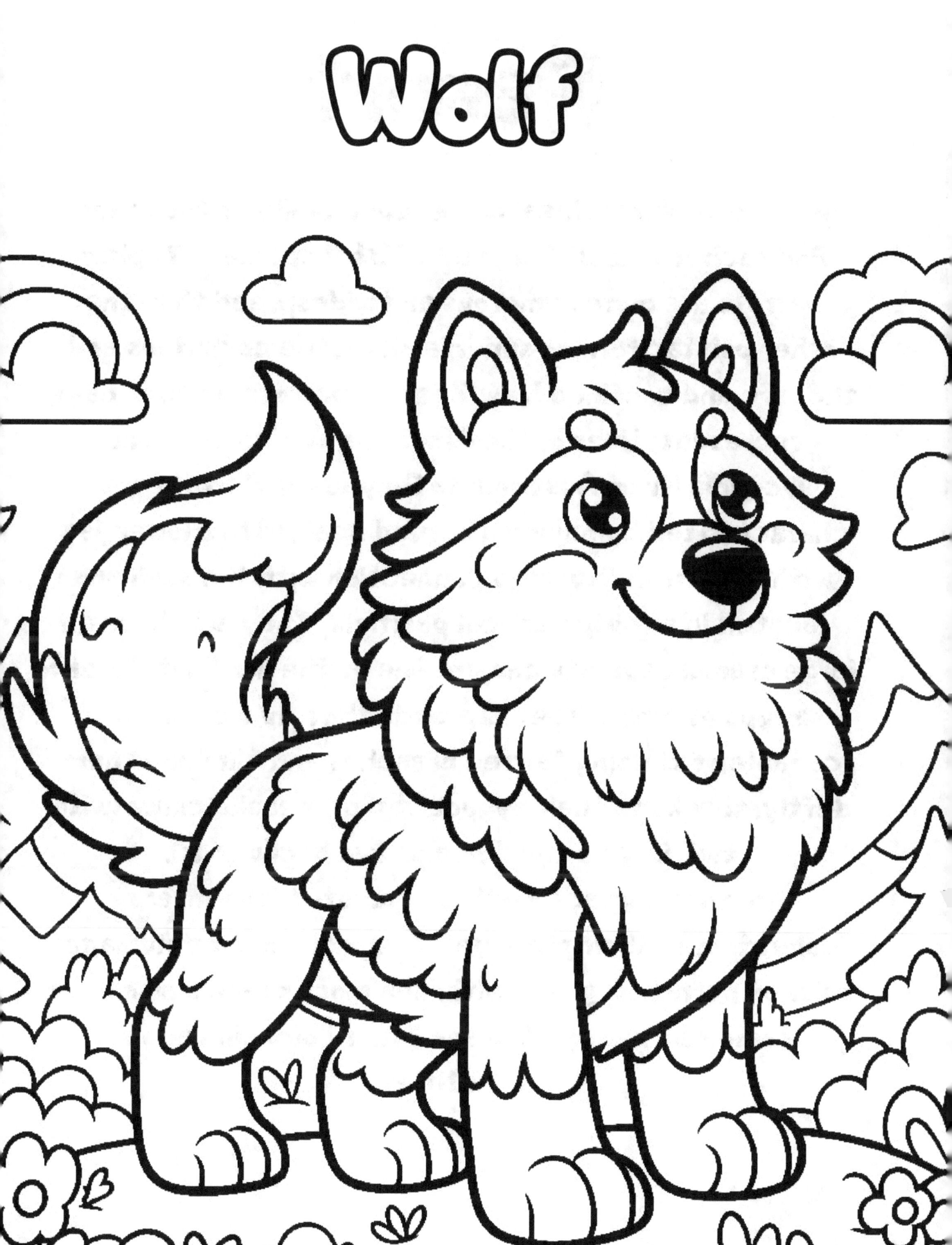

Parrot

Parrots (Psittacoidea) are a superfamily of the order Psittaciformes, with a total of 369 species. Typical parrots are more numerous and widespread than the other psittaciformes superfamilies, the cockatoos and the rare and confined New Zealand parrots, as they have representatives in the Americas, Africa, Asia and Oceania (from Australia to Polynesia). Parrots are characterized by having a curved beak, with a lower jaw with some mobility in its connection with the skull and located in a fairly vertical position. They also have a large cranial capacity and are one of the most intelligent groups of birds. They are birds that fly well and are capable of clinging to tree branches and climbing them deftly, thanks to their zygodactyl prehensile claws (with two fingers forward and two backwards).

Another characteristic of parrots is the intense coloration of their plumage. The predominant plumage color of parrots is green, although most species also have some red, blue, yellow and other colors in various quantities.

Parrot

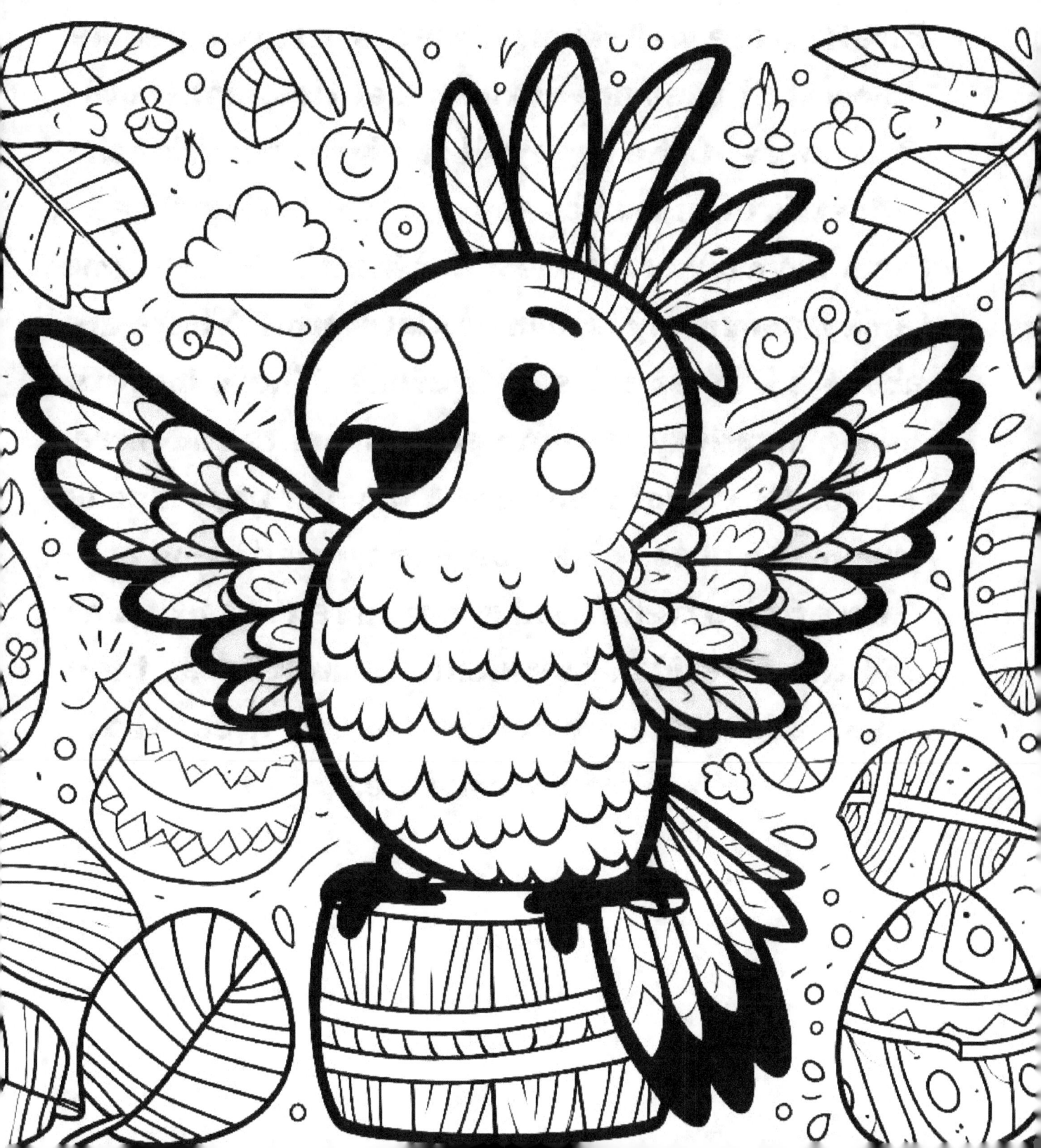

Firefly

Fireflies are well-known insects, but few people know that they are actually beetles, night-owl members of the lampyrid family (Lampyridae). Most fireflies have wings, which distinguishes them from other luminescent insects in the same family, commonly known as glowworms. There are about 2,000 species of fireflies. These insects live in a variety of warm environments and more temperate regions, and are a familiar presence on summer nights. Fireflies love humidity and are therefore often found in humid regions of Asia and the American continent. In drier areas they can be found near humid or swampy areas that retain moisture.

Firefly

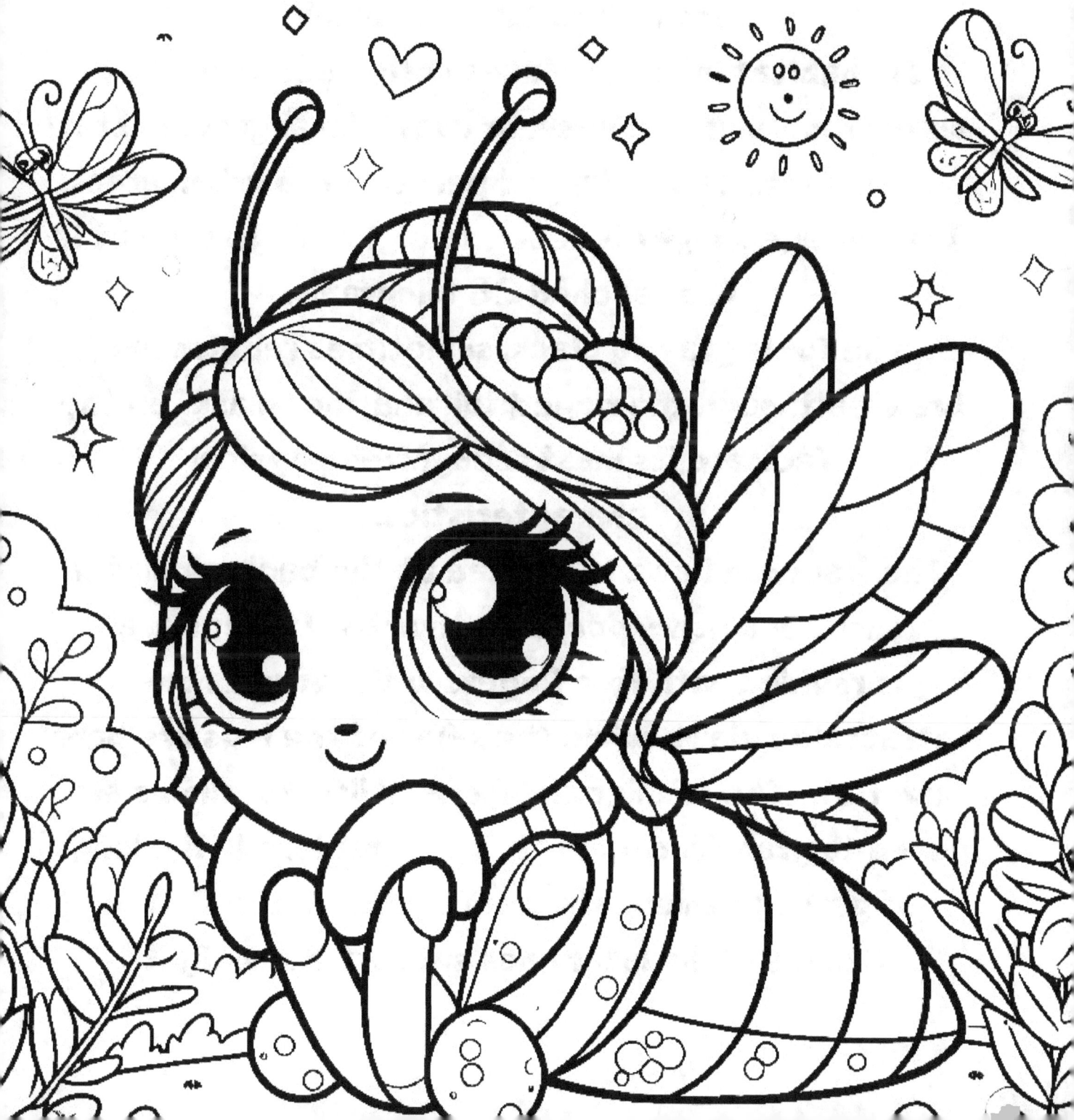

Raccoon

The Raccoon is a mammal of the Procyonidae family and originally from America (its distribution ranges from Canada to Panama).

Its habitat includes places with trees, close to a water reservoir or course, or coastal mangroves; It is a species that has adapted perfectly to urban areas. Its average weight is seven to eight kilograms, but it has reached 28 kilograms.

The fur is gray to black, sometimes reddish and brown, although the ringed tail and the "mask" on the face are its most recognized physical characteristics.

The Raccoon has a wide head at the back, a pointed snout and non-opposable thumbs; Its legs are provided with five fingers with curved, non-retractable claws, while the soles of the legs are bare and flat. The smaller and more skillful forelimbs are used to grab food (in fact, it is considered "the king of garbage thieves" in some cities in the United States); The later ones support the weight.

Raccoon

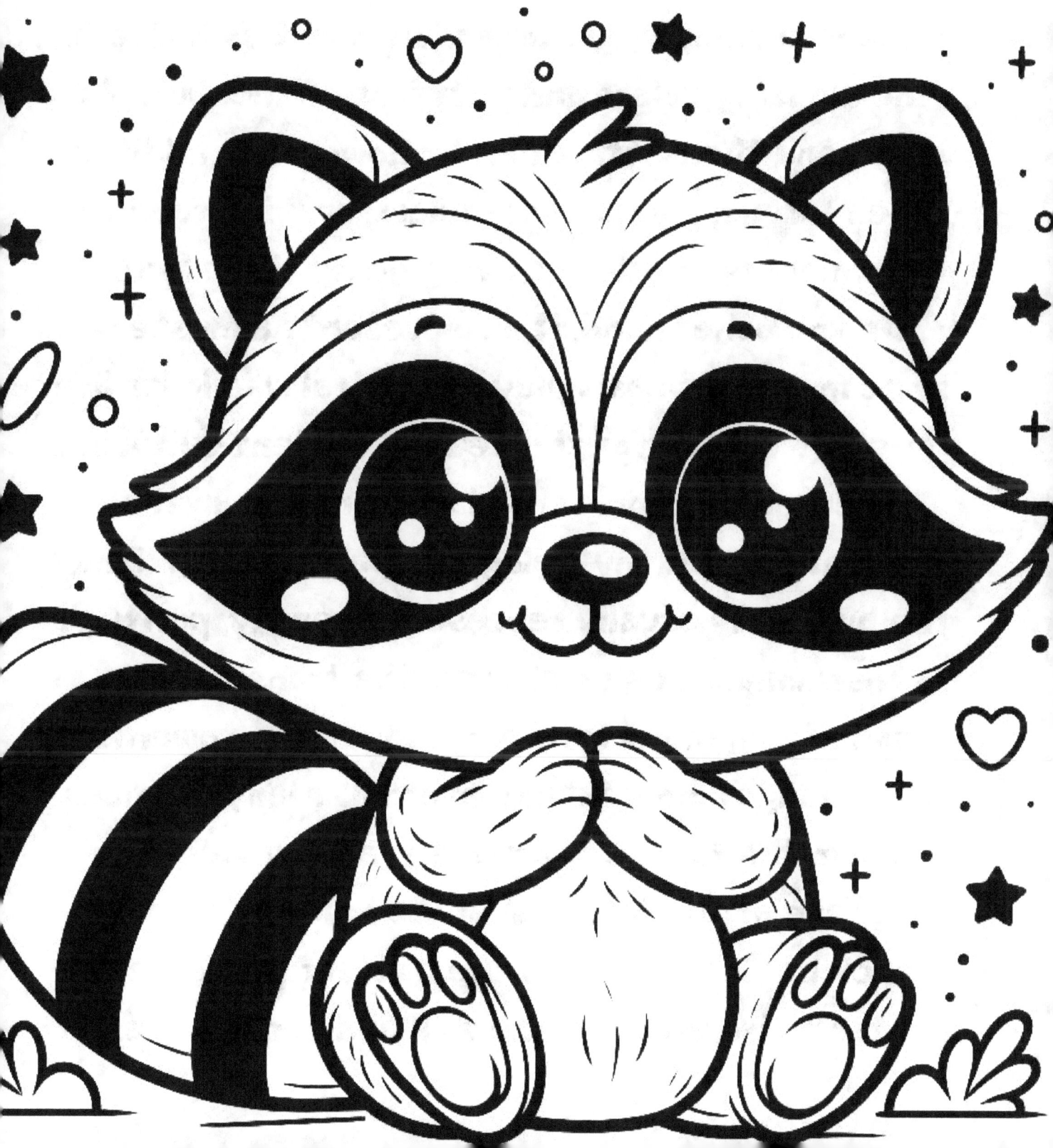

Butterfly

Butterflies have attracted the attention of humans since ancient times. In part this is due to the amazing colors and patterns of the diurnals' wings, and their attraction to flowers. In addition, their larvae, called caterpillars, provide food to numerous species of living beings in nature.

On the other hand, it also presents a mystery since metamorphosis plays a central role in its life cycle. Perhaps for this reason, ancient cultures reserved an important place for them in their imagination and mythology. In various traditions, the butterfly usually represents beauty, purity or harmony, but also change, the transition of something imperfect and temporary, towards something wonderful and eternal. Many religions saw in the fate of butterflies an equivalent to the fate of the human soul. So much so that the ancient Greeks called the butterfly psyche, a term also used for the soul and conscience.

Butterfly

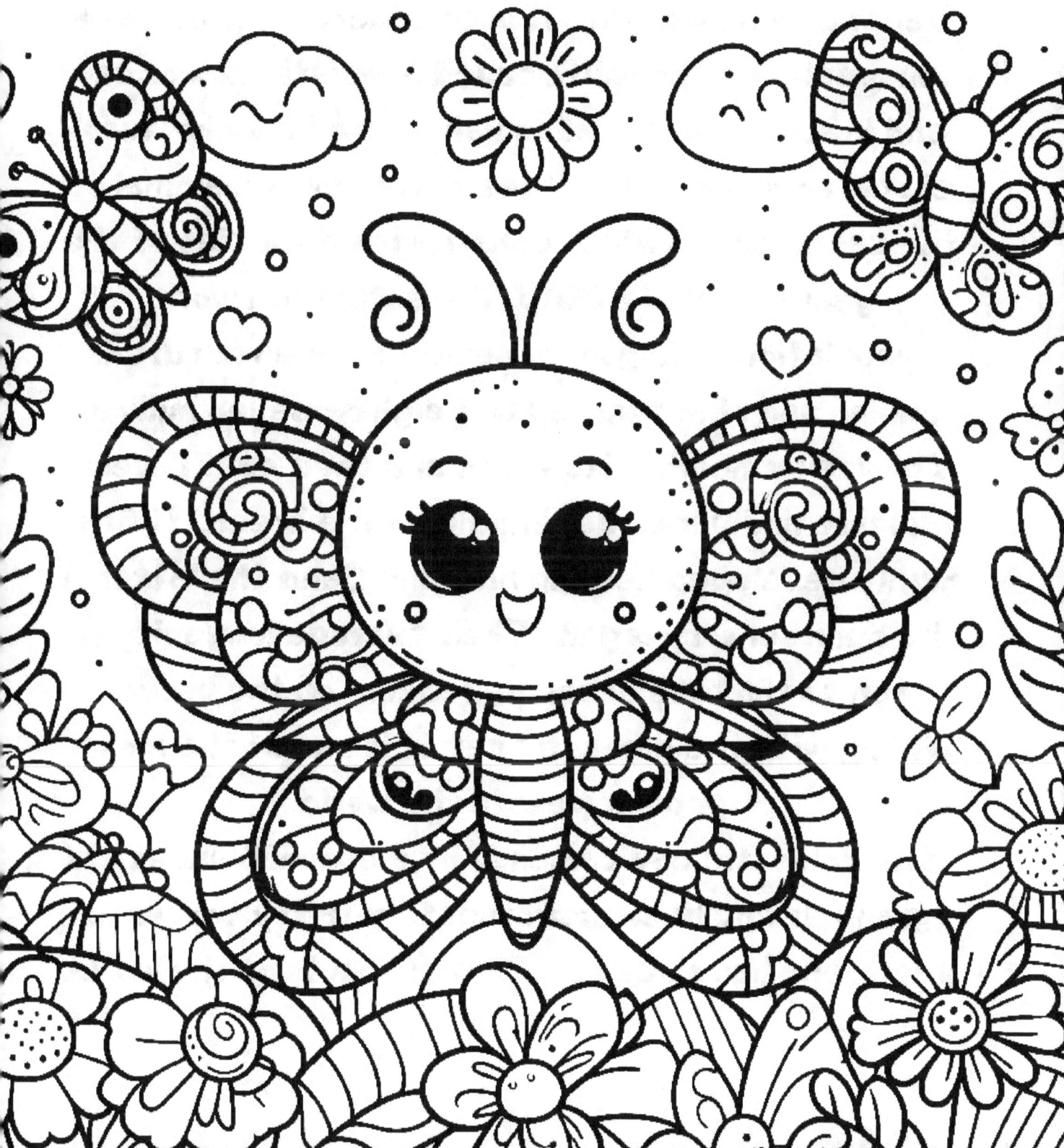

Dog

The dog (Canis familiaris or Canis lupus familiaris, depending on whether it is considered a species or subspecies of the wolf), called domestic dog or can, and in some places colloquially called chucho, tuso, choco, among others; It is a carnivorous mammal of the canid family, which constitutes a species of the genus Canis. In 2013, the estimated world population of dogs was between seven hundred million and nine hundred and eighty-seven million. Its size (or height), its shape and their coat is very diverse and varies depending on the breed. It has highly developed hearing and smell, and the latter is its main sensory organ. Their average longevity is ten to thirteen years, depending on the breed. Along with the domestic cat, it is one of the most popular pets in the world.

The domestic dog comes from a common ancestral group dating back approximately thirty thousand years, and has since spread to all parts of the world.

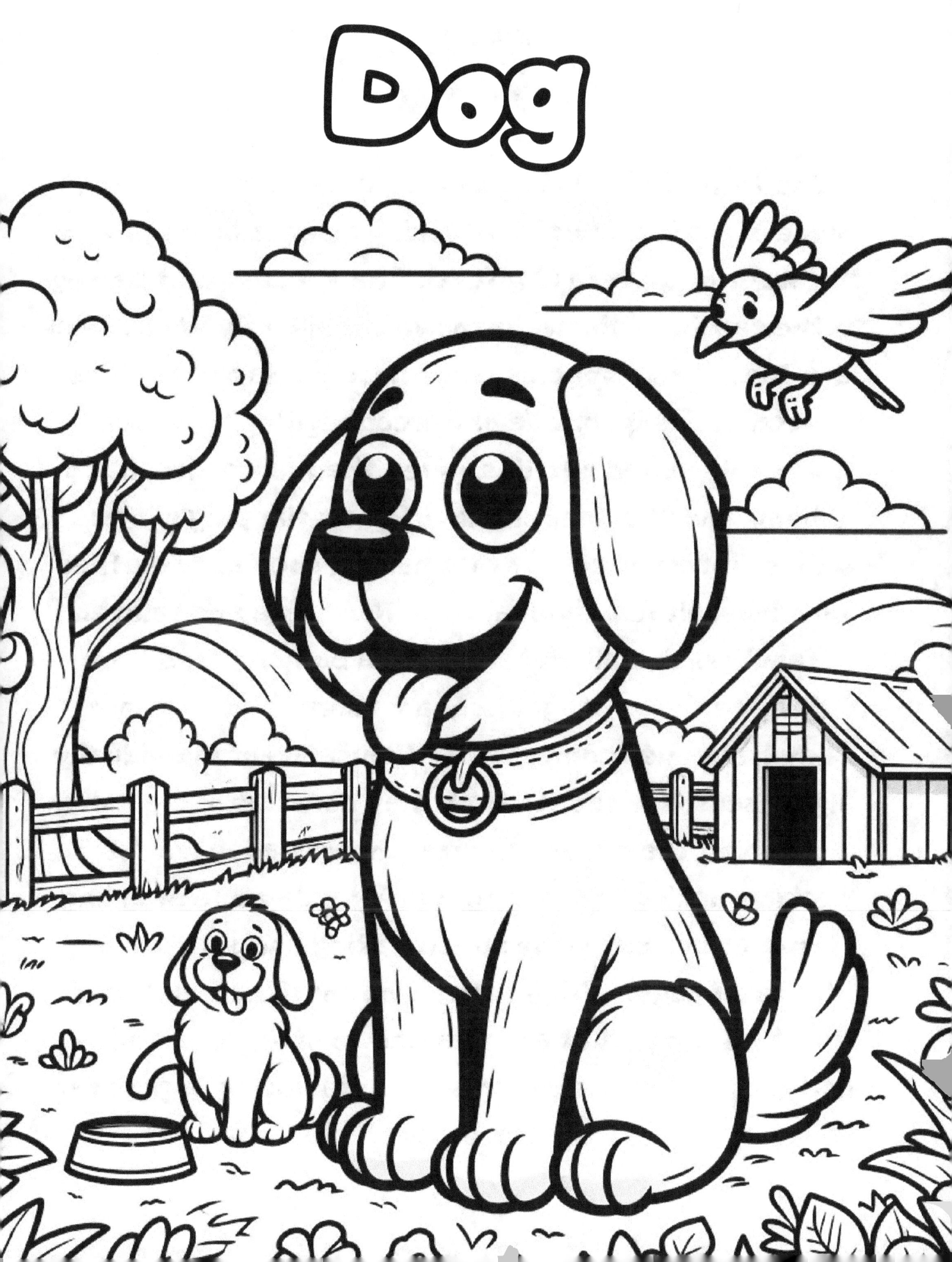

Fly

The term fly (from the Latin musca) is the common name of various species of flying insects belonging to the order of diptera (Diptera). The species that belong to the family of the well-known common fly (Muscidae) are flies; Some species from closely related families, such as Calliphoridae or Sarcophagidae, are more commonly called botflies, given their large size, hairy body, and the deeper hum of their flapping wings. Other diptera receive other names, such as horseflies and mosquitoes. Typical flies (Muscidae and related families), like all diptera, have a body divided into three regions or tagmas: head, thorax and abdomen. They have eyes composed of thousands of individually light-sensitive facets that they constantly clean by rubbing their paws, and mouthparts adapted for sucking, licking or piercing; No fly is capable of biting or chewing, but many species sting and suck blood (hematophagy). They have two functional wings and two hind wings that are reduced to structures called halteres or rockers, which act as stabilizing organs for movement.

Fly

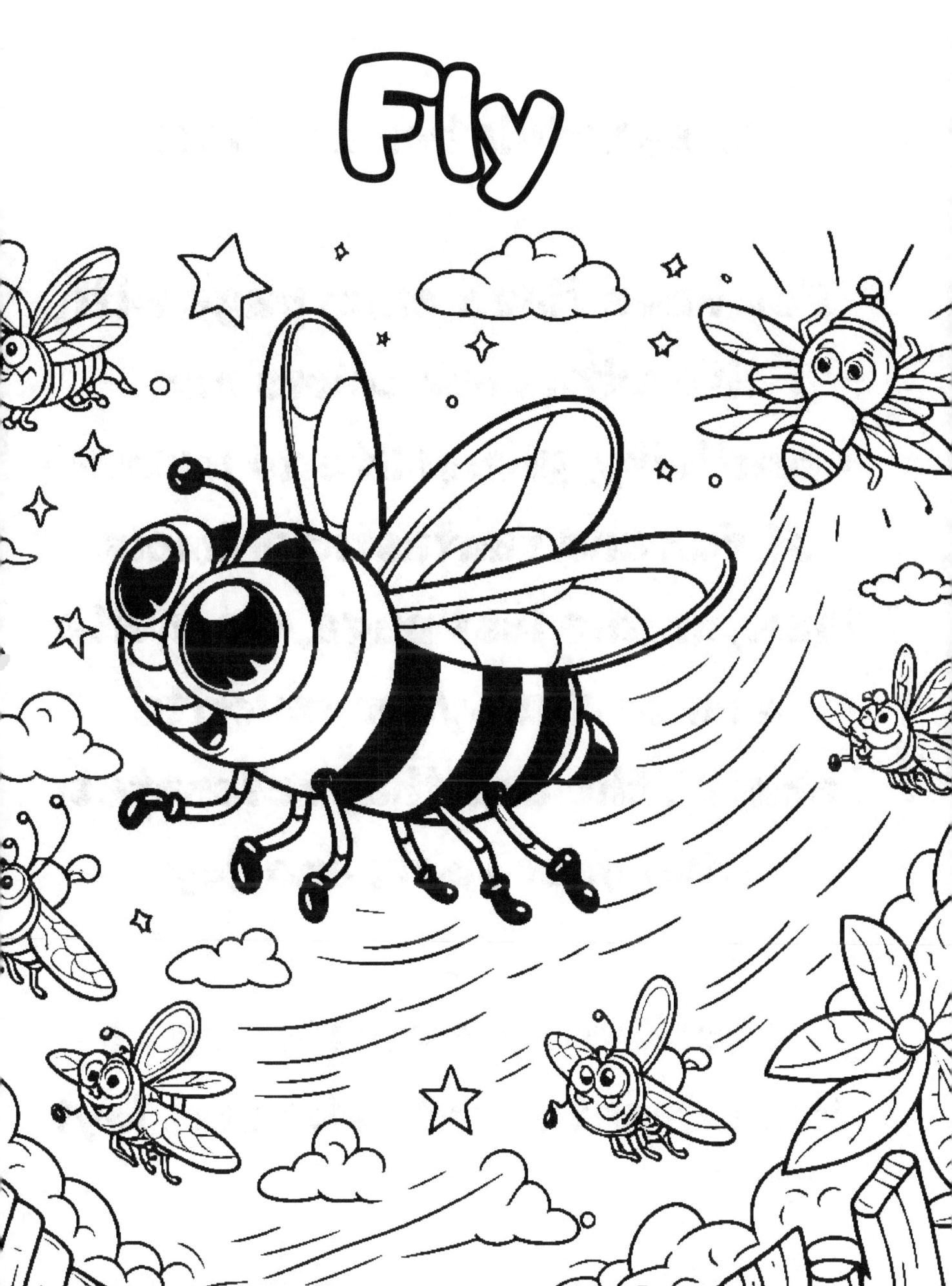

Congratulations, artist!

You have filled each page with life with your colors and creativity, giving life to a world of fun and fantastic animals. Now, on the last page, we invite you to draw your favorite animal, the one that resonates with your spirit and joy.

Thank you for embarking on this adventure of color and joy!

www.ingramcontent.com/pod-product-compliance
Lightning Source LLC
Chambersburg PA
CBHW082344220526
45470CB00008B/2641